When NLP Meets LLM

Neural Approaches to Context-based Conversational Question Answering

Munazza Zaib, Quan Z. Sheng,
Wei Emma Zhang, and Adnan Mahmood

CRC Press
Taylor & Francis Group
Boca Raton London New York

CRC Press is an imprint of the
Taylor & Francis Group, an **informa** business

First edition published 2026
by CRC Press
2385 NW Executive Center Drive, Suite 320, Boca Raton FL 33431

and by CRC Press
4 Park Square, Milton Park, Abingdon, Oxon, OX14 4RN

CRC Press is an imprint of Taylor & Francis Group, LLC

© 2026 **Munazza Zaib**, **Quan Z. Sheng**, **Wei Emma Zhang** and **Adnan Mahmood**

ISBN: 978-1-032-97084-4 (hbk)
ISBN: 978-1-032-97079-0 (pbk)
ISBN: 978-1-003-59206-8 (ebk)

DOI: 10.1201/9781003592068

Typeset in Nimbus font
by KnowledgeWorks Global Ltd.

Publisher's note: This book has been prepared from camera-ready copy provided by the authors.

To Talha, my rock, and to Farzan, my little spark—
your love, laughter, and belief in me have carried me
through the toughest days and made the good ones even
brighter.
This journey would never have been the same without you.

Munazza Zaib

To my mum for her unconditional and everlasting love. To
my wife, Stella, and my daughters, Fiona and Phoebe, for
their love and support.

Quan Z. Sheng

To my beloved family, for walking beside me and offering
unwavering support and unconditional love.

Wei E. Zhang

To my loving wife, Fatima, and beloved children, Rafay,
Talha, and Anna, for their love and support.

Adnan Mahmood

Contents

List of Figures

List of Tables

Authors

Munazza Zaib holds a PhD from Macquarie University, Sydney, Australia and is currently a Postdoctoral Research Fellow at the Department of Human Centred Computing, Faculty of Information Technology, Monash University, Melbourne, Australia. Before starting at Monash University, Munazza has spent a considerable number of years in the academic and research settings of Macquarie University. Her research interests include Information Retrieval, Natural Language Processing, their applications in Conversational Question Answering and Intelligent Dialogue Agents, etc. Munazza, besides, serves as a Reviewer and on the Technical Program Committees of a number of reputed International Conferences. She was selected to participate in the 11th Heidelberg Laureate Forum held in September 2024 in Heidelberg, Germany. She is a member of the IEEE and the ACM.

Quan Z. Sheng is a Distinguished Professor and Head of School of Computing at Macquarie University, Australia. Before moving to Macquarie University, Michael spent 10 years at School of Computer Science, the University of Adelaide, serving in a number of senior leadership roles including Interim Head and Deputy Head of School of Computer Science. Michael holds a PhD degree in computer science from the University of New South Wales (UNSW) and did his post-doc as a research scientist at CSIRO ICT Centre. From 1999 to 2001, Michael worked at UNSW as a visiting research fellow. Prior to that, he spent 6 years as a Senior Software Engineer in industries. Prof. Sheng is ranked by Microsoft

Academic as one of the Most Impactful Authors in Services Computing (ranked Top 5 of All Time worldwide) in 2021 and by ScholarGPS as one of the Highly Ranked Scholars in Web Information System (ranked Top 5 Lifetime worldwide) in 2025. He is the recipient of the AMiner Most Influential Scholar Award on IoT (2007–2017), ARC (Australian Research Council) Future Fellowship (2014), Chris Wallace Award for Outstanding Research Contribution (2012), and Microsoft Research Fellowship (2003). Prof Michael Sheng was the Vice Chair of the Executive Committee of the IEEE Technical Community on Services Computing (IEEE TCSVC, 2022–2024) and has been a member of the ACS (Australian Computing Society) Technical Advisory Board on IoT since 2019.

Wei Emma Zhang is a Senior Lecturer and Associate Head of People and Culture at the School of Computer and Mathematical Sciences, and a Researcher at the Australian Institute for Machine Learning, The University of Adelaide. She received her PhD degree in Computer Science from the University of Adelaide. Dr Zhang is the ARC Industry Early Career Research Fellow 2024–2027. She is the SA 2024 Young Tall Poppy Award recipient and the Women in AI APAC 2024 award finalist. Dr Zhang's research interests include Document Summarization, Artificial Intelligence of Things and Machine Learning. She has over 140 publications as edited books and proceedings, refereed book chapters, and technical papers in journals and conferences. Her PhD thesis had been published by Springer as a monograph. Wei is the top 100 authors worldwide, ranked by field-weighted citation impact, in the SciVal topic for Network Security. Her first-authored journal article was recognized as the #2 most outstanding article ever published in ACM Transactions on Intelligent Systems and Technology (TIST; Q1, impact factor [IF] 5.443; h-index 71), selected by the journal EiC. Besides, Dr Zhang has 6 years of industry working experience in multiple roles and has strong industry engagements. She is a member of ACM, IEEE, and ACS.

Adnan Mahmood possesses a PhD in Computer Science and is a Lecturer in Computing—IoT and Networking at the School of Computing, Macquarie University, Sydney, Australia. Before moving to Macquarie University, Adnan has spent a considerable number of years in both academic and research settings of the Republic of Ireland, Malaysia, Pakistan, and the People's Republic of China. His research interests include, but are not limited to, the Internet of Things, Internet of Vehicles, Trust Management, Software-Defined Networking, and the Next Generation Heterogeneous Wireless Networks. His extensive publication list includes refereed book chapters; journal articles published in prestigious venues, including but not limited to, the ACM Computing Surveys, IEEE Transactions on Knowledge and Data Engineering, IEEE Transactions on Intelligent Transportation Systems, IEEE Transactions on Network and Service Management, ACM Transactions on Sensor Networks, ACM Transactions on Cyber-Physical Systems, and Scientific Reports (Nature Portfolio); and papers in highly reputed international conferences, including but not limited to, International Joint Conference on Artificial Intelligence, AAAI Conference on Artificial Intelligence, International Conference on Web Services, and International Conference on Service-Oriented Computing. Adnan, besides, serves on the Technical Program Committees of a number of reputed international conferences. He is a member of the IEEE, IET, and ACM.

CHAPTER 1

Introduction

Designing an intelligent dialog system that not only matches or surpasses a human's level in carrying out an interactive conversation, but also answers questions on a variety of topics, i.e., ranging from recent news about National Aeronautics and Space Administration (NASA) to a biography of a famous political leader, has been one of the major goals in the field of artificial intelligence (AI) [8]. A quickly increasing number of research papers prove the promising potential and the growing interest of researchers from both academia and industry in conversational AI (ConvAI). ConvAI constitutes an integral part of Natural User Interfaces(NLIs) [8] and is attracting attention from researchers in Information Retrieval (IR), Natural Language Processing (NLP), and Deep Learning (DL) communities [9].

The field of ConvAI can be segregated into three groups namely, (i) *task-oriented dialog systems* that are required to perform tasks on the users' behalf such as making a reservation in a restaurant or scheduling an event, (ii) *chat-oriented dialog systems* that need to carry out a natural and interactive conversation with the users, and (iii) *QA dialog systems* that are responsible to provide clear and concise answers to the users' questions based on information deduced from different data sources such as text documents or knowledge bases. The examples of each of the aforementioned categories are

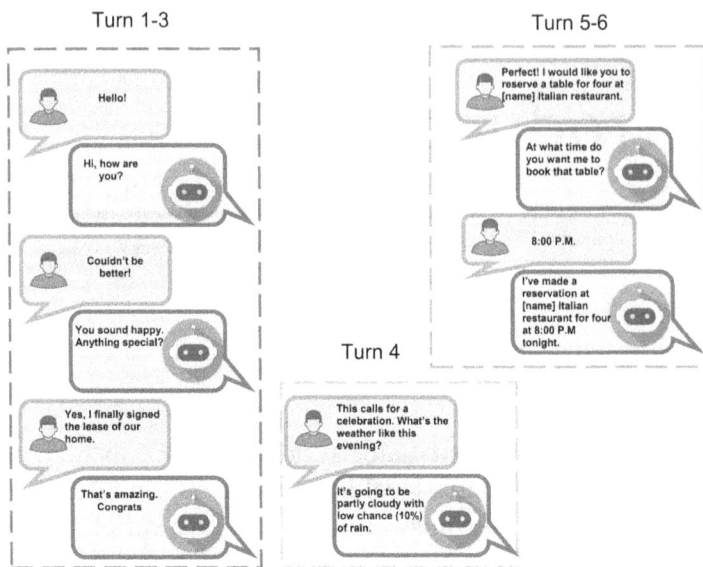

FIGURE 1.1 Categorizations of ConvAI. Turns 1–3 depict a chat-oriented dialog system, turn 4 portrays the element of the QA dialog system, and turn 5-6 reflects the task-oriented conversation.

given in Figure 1.1. The conversation shown in Figure 1.1 comprises multiple turns and each turn consists of a question and an answer [20].

The chat-oriented and task-oriented dialog systems have been well-researched topics resulting in many successful dialog agents such as Amazon Alexa[1], Apple Siri[2], and Microsoft Cortana[3]. However, QA dialog systems are fairly new and still require extensive research. Many QA challenges have been identified and initial solutions have been proposed [19, 13, 11, 21, 29, 6, 2, 22], giving the rise of ConvQA. ConvQA techniques form the building blocks of QA

---

[1]https://www.amazon.com.au/b?node=5425666051
[2]https://www.apple.com/au/siri/
[3]https://www.microsoft.com/en-us/cortana

dialog systems. The idea behind ConvQA is to ask the machine to answer a question based on the provided passage and this, in turn, has the potential to revolutionize the way humans interact with the machines. However, this interaction could turn into a multi-turn conversation if a user requires more detailed information about the question. The notion of ConvQA can be thought of as a simplified but concrete conversational search setting [18], wherein the system returns one correct answer to a user's question instead of a list of relevant documents or links as is the case with traditional search engines. The top search engine companies such as Microsoft and Google have incorporated ConvQA into their mobile-based search engines (also known as *digital assistants*) to improve the users' experience when interacting with them.

Due to the recent rise in demand for digital personal assistants, organizations and businesses are shifting their information-seeking activities to conversational interfaces. Apart from being utilized in professional setups, these agents are also used by individuals for entertainment purposes and even as an emotional support system [7]. Although existing intelligent agents are smart enough to carry out basic tasks, i.e., placing an order or setting a reminder on a user's behalf and can even chit-chat informally, these still struggle with carrying out a long engaging conversation consisting of multiple turns with complex information needs [16, 25, 24, 17]. These digital personal agents play a key role in providing easy interfaces to the users for their information needs. However, these systems still require a lot of research to be fully able to carry out conversational search.

1.1 CONVERSATIONAL SEARCH: BRIDGING THE GAP BETWEEN USERS AND INFORMATION

Conversational search can be regarded as the broader category of ConvQA [18, 17]. Conversational search sets the stage by retrieving relevant information, and

Conversational
Search

Conversational
Question Answering

**Conversational
Machine Reading
Comprehension**

Sequential KB-QA

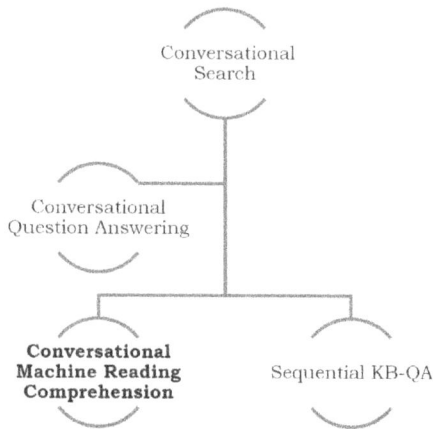

FIGURE 1.2 Hierarchy of conversational search. The main focus of the book, i.e., conversational machine reading comprehension is represented in bold in the figure.

ConvQA builds upon this foundation to provide accurate and contextually appropriate answers to users' queries. The task of ConvQA can be further categorized into Sequential Knowledge-Based Question Answering (Sequential KB-QA) and conversational machine reading comprehension (CMRC). The main focus of this book is the task of CMRC[4] as highlighted in Figure 1.2. Conversational search can be carried out by utilizing different sources such as knowledge bases and textual passages [15]. This research work focuses on text-based documents in machine reading comprehension (MRC) and addresses the challenges pertinent to it. It is worth noting that conversational context plays a central role throughout the dialog/search process [18, 17, 25]. Thus, the primary emphasis of the book lies in the selection and modeling of relevant context effectively, as a significant step toward the progression of conversational search.

A typical conversation encapsulates a number of turns. Usually, a user initiates the conversation with a specific

---

[4]ConvQA and CMRC are used interchangeably in the book except in Chapter 2.

information need in mind, and then the system tries to look for the right answer to the question by asking follow-up questions to fill in the missing information, if any [1, 30]. This conversation could shift to a different but related topic by the user, thereby entering into the next turn. The example shown in Table 1.1 formulates the task of ConvQA and depicts that follow-up questions could be related to their conversation history. It is entirely essential for the system to model the conversational context effectively to understand and help the users with their information needs. Therefore, the research work addresses issues like filling in the missing information in incomplete or ambiguous questions, relevant history selection and modeling, and expanding the task of ConvQA to open-domain conversational question answering (OD-ConvQA).

The remaining chapter is organized as follows. Section 1.1 delineates the research objectives and motivation of the book. Section 1.2 identifies the research questions based on the research motivation and discusses the contributions of the book toward addressing the challenges identified. In the end, Section 1.3 provides an overview of the book's organization chapter by chapter. sectionResearch Challenges and Motivation The task of ConvQA is carried out in multiple turns, wherein, a user expresses his information needs through a series of utterances with incomplete context [5]. This incomplete context hinders the ConvQA model from fully interpreting a given question, thereby, resulting in no answer or inaccurate answer span in some cases. This underlines the significance of having the correct context pertinent to the conversation to be better able to grasp the meaning of question-at-hand. Thus, the research challenges and motivation of this book can be described in the sequel.

1.1.1 Incomplete and Ambiguous Questions

Originating from ELIZA [23] in the last decade, the field of ConvQA has made a rapid development owing to its exciting

TABLE 1.1 An Example of Information-Seeking Dialog from QuAC [4]

	Topic: Geographic Distribution and Population
ID	**Conversation**
Q1	Where is Malayali located?
A1	30,803,747 speakers of Malayalam in Kerala, making up 93.2% of the total number of Malayalam speakers in India.
Q2	What other languages are spoken there?
A2	33,015,420 spoke the standard dialects, 19,643 spoke the Yerava dialect, and 31,329 spoke non-standard regional variations like Eranadan.
Q3	What else is this place known for?
A3	World Malayalee Council, the organization working ... embarked upon a project for making a data bank of the diaspora.
Q4	Were they ever successful in doing this?
A4	CANNOTANSWER
Q5	Is this population still growing?
A5	In 2010, the Census of Population of Singapore reported that there were 26,348 Malayalees in Singapore.
Q6	Is the country thriving?
A6	*To be answered.*

Related terms and co-dependencies are highlighted in the same color. Q2 does not follow up on Q1 and shows *topic shift* from Malyalis to Kerala, whereas, Q5 shows *topic return* similar to that of Q1, Q2, Q3, Q4, and Q5 talk about the state and its people making them related, whereas Q6 talks about the country making it unrelated to the previous questions.

prospects of revolutionizing the world. The topic continues to pique the curiosity of the researchers, and as a result, we see several research works being translated and used in both industries as well as our daily lives[5,6]. These intelligent agents are required to resolve the co-references and

---

[5]https://en.wikipedia.org/wiki/Xiaoice
[6]https://www.amazon.science/tag/alexa

conversational dependencies to comprehend the current question. Most often, the follow-up questions put forward by the users are implicit and missing complete information. Users posing incomplete and ambiguous questions in ConvQA setting can introduce several challenges that impact system performance and user experience. The issues include, but are not limited to:

1. **Unclear Intent:** Incomplete questions may lack clarity regarding a user's intent, thereby making it challenging for the ConvQA system to discern the specific information a user is seeking.

2. **Contextual Dependencies:** ConvQA systems heavily rely on context to understand and answer questions. Incomplete or ambiguous questions may disrupt the contextual flow thus making it harder for the system to generate appropriate responses.

3. **Difficulty in Information Retrieval:** Incomplete questions may lack essential keywords, thereby impacting a system's ability to retrieve relevant information. Ambiguities can further complicate the information retrieval process, in turn, yielding less accurate results.

4. **Need for Clarification Prompts:** ConvQA systems may need to prompt users for clarification when faced with incomplete or ambiguous questions. This disrupts the conversational flow and requires additional user effort.

Addressing these issues requires identifying the missing information and filling it in to paint a complete picture of the current question to the ConvQA system.

1.1.2 Relevant History Selection

The task of ConvQA has gained much attention recently as it is very close to how humans seek information [10]. In a typical use-case of ConvQA, the user initiates the conversation by asking a question regarding a particular information need. The system then tries to look for the required information by interacting with the user iteratively. These iterations encompass the system asking questions proactively to better understand a user's information need and retrieving the answers based on the feedback provided by the user. The user sometimes puts forward a follow-up question with related but new information need and enters the next *'turn'* of the ConvQA process. In order to track and understand the nature of a user's information request, the model should be able to maintain the conversational context and be able to use it when needed. For instance, the example in Table 1.1 shows the essence of the information need in the conversational context by highlighting the co-dependent turns in the conversation. However, adding the entire context as a part of the input to the model may bring noise to the system and result in the degradation of a model's performance. For example, to answer Q5, the model needs only Q1, thereby, making it irrelevant to add all the previous turns. Thus, selecting and modeling relevant history turns in the conversational search system is an important aspect of addressing the changing information needs across the turns for the researchers. The book follows the definition of ConvQA formulated by Reddy et al. [20] and Choi et al. [4], wherein the model needs to predict the answer span given the passage, current question, and the conversational history turns.

1.1.3 Open-Domain Conversational Question Answering

A major shortcoming of the current ConvQA setting is that it assumes that the passage is always provided with the current question and the answer is extracted from it [4, 20]. However, the simplification of the task neglects the role of retrieval in the conversational search. To address this limitation, we continue and expand our work from ConvQA to the OD-ConvQA setting, wherein the model learns to retrieve the relevant passages first before attempting to select the correct answer span.

The task of OD-ConvQA requires an additional step of retrieving the relevant passages first. These retrieved passages are then passed on to the reader for the selection of the correct answer span. Since the passage pool could be huge consisting of thousands of candidate documents, it makes it difficult for the model to jointly encode the passages and question together [3]. The dominant technique to tackle the challenge is dense retrieval [12], which encodes a query and documents as dense representations separately and performs a nearest neighbor search that is efficient and scalable to millions of documents. However, utilizing dense passage retrieval (DPR) also needs to consider the conversational context and the structure which the existing approaches fail to consider when designing an OD-ConvQA-based model. To address the issue, the role of DPR, given a curated conversational context and how it affects the answering performance of the model, is studied.

1.2 RESEARCH QUESTIONS AND CONTRIBUTIONS OF THE BOOK

In light of the aforementioned research bottlenecks, this book intends to address these research questions. Specifically, an overview of the technical research questions and chapters pertinent to them is shown in Figure 1.3.

RQ 1: To what extent have recent advancements in ConvQA systems addressed the challenges pertinent to multi-turn interaction and context modeling?

This research work endeavors to offer a comprehensive review of current research trends in ConvQA by primarily drawing insights from the recently reviewed literature. Accordingly, Chapter 2 [26] delves into various approaches employed to tackle the ConvQA task, and outlines the strengths and weaknesses of each method. Subsequently, it provides a

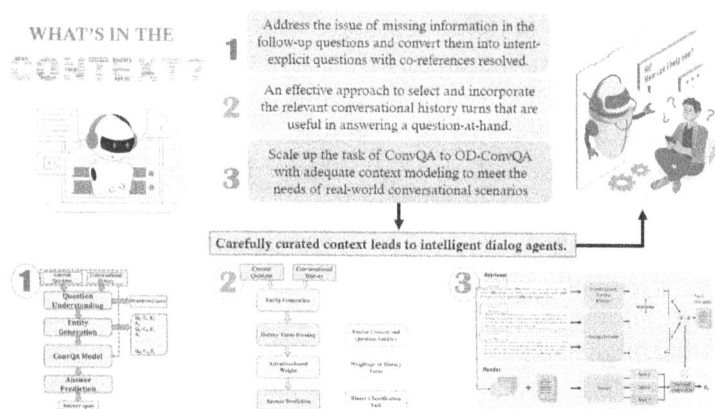

FIGURE 1.3 From investigation to book's technical chapters.

detailed exploration of the conversational datasets utilized for simulation and experimentation. The study identifies potential avenues for future research, in particular, those pertaining to context incorporation. The findings of the chapter reveal a noticeable shift from single-turn to multi-turn QA, in a bid to showcase the evolving landscape of ConvAI from diverse perspectives.

RQ 2: How to address the issue of missing information in the follow-up questions and convert them into intent-explicit questions from the implicit ones by resolving the co-references between the conversational turns so that the ConvQA system can interpret the information needs of a user better?

The exploration in Chapter 3 [27] outlines a strategy for addressing the challenge of incomplete or ambiguous follow-up questions. While humans effortlessly relate current questions to previous context, machines require the resolution of co-references to enhance their understanding. Our proposed solution involves capturing structured representations from the context to serve as an additional cue for the model, thus supplementing the input and improving comprehension of the question. Integrating these structured representations with incomplete questions proves more effective than rewriting questions from scratch, in turn, providing a valuable means to fill in the missing information.

RQ 3: How to effectively select and incorporate the relevant conversational history turns that are useful in answering a question-at-hand and study the effect of filtering out the irrelevant context on the performance of the model?

Chapter 4 [27] endeavors to explore an approach for effectively incorporating conversational context into the system to enhance its ability to comprehend questions and select the correct answer span. The model utilizes BART [14] to learn and generate context and question entities. Turns that share similar entities with the current question are retained for constituting hard history selection. Attention weights for each turn are calculated and the turns are included in the input order based on these weights to form the basis for *soft history selection*. Finally, the term classification layer is added at the top and is used to emphasize crucial terms in the model.

RQ 4: How to scale up the task of ConvQA to OD-ConvQA to meet the needs of real-world conversational scenarios where the topic/passages are not always provided with the current question and the curated context can be subsequently incorporated to better guide the retriever about the passage retrieval process?

The motivation driving the investigation in Chapter 5 [28] stems from the limitation in ConvQA, wherein a passage is necessary to answer a question. Real-life scenarios often differ from this since a passage is not always provided with the question. To address this challenge, we delve into the task of OD-ConvQA which involves initially retrieving passages and subsequently selecting the correct answer span.

The process begins by filtering out irrelevant turns. Once the relevant context is identified, the next step is to narrow down the passages that are pertinent to those turns. Utilizing contrastive learning, passages are retrieved, minimizing the distance between similar passages and pushing irrelevant passages farther in the embedding vector space. After collecting similar and relevant passages, the reader then selects the correct answer span.

1.3 BOOK ORGANIZATION

The remainder of the book is organized into the following five chapters:

Chapter 2: Understanding the Essence of Conversational Question Answering
This chapter offers a comprehensive analysis of the field of ConvQA. It starts with a discussion on the transition from the task of QA to ConvQA and how they differ from each other followed by a discussion regarding the categorization of ConvQA at different levels. The chapter then introduces sequential KB-QA and CMRC with a detailed discussion of different techniques employed in each module of a CMRC-based architecture. The chapter then highlights different ConvQA-based datasets and their unique characteristics. It also briefly explains the data collection process for each dataset. The chapter ends with a discussion of the potential directions where the task of ConvQA can be employed.

Chapter 3: Resolving Dependencies in ConvQA
This chapter is an attempt to address the issue of dependencies within incomplete or ambiguous follow-up questions using structured representations. The proposed model, **ConvQA using Structured Representations (CONVSR)**, first selects the relevant turns by calculating soft-cosine similarity. Once the irrelevant context is filtered out, the model

generates intermediate structured representations that can be provided as an additional cue to the model to better understand a question at hand.

Chapter 4: Dynamic History Selection for ConvQA
Chapter 4 proposes a dynamic history selection process that is more intuitive rather than just using the similarity functions. The proposed model, **Dynamic History Selection in ConvQA** (DHS-ConvQA), follows a series of steps to filter and align the relevant history turns so that the model can benefit from the curated input. In the end, the model uses a binary term classification layer to highlight the important terms for the model to focus on.

Chapter 5: History Modeling for OD-ConvQA
This chapter is an effort to extend the task of ConvQA to a more realistic setting of OD-ConvQA where a passage is not always given with the current question. The proposed model, **Dense Passage Retrieval in Conversational Question Answering** (DPR-ConvQA), first selects a subset of relevant turns to guide the retrieval process of the passages from a huge collection. The model then uses a contrastive learning strategy to minimize the distance between related passages to help the reader select the correct answer span.

Chapter 6: Conclusion
This chapter summarizes the book findings and the research challenges addressed by the same. Moreover, some future research directions pertinent to the topic are elaborated.

References

[1] Mohammad Aliannejadi et al. "Asking Clarifying Questions in Open-Domain Information-Seeking Conversations". In: *Proceedings of the 42nd International ACM SIGIR Conference on Research and Develop-*

ment in Information Retrieval (SIGIR). Ed. by Benjamin Piwowarski et al. 2019, pp. 475–484.

[2] Junwei Bao et al. "Constraint-Based Question Answering with Knowledge Graph". In: *Proceedings of the 26th International Conference on Computational Linguistics (COLING)*. 2016, pp. 2503–2514.

[3] Danqi Chen et al. "Reading Wikipedia to Answer Open-Domain Questions". In: *Proceedings of the 55th Annual Meeting of the Association for Computational Linguistics (ACL)*. 2017, pp. 1870–1879.

[4] Eunsol Choi et al. "QuAC: Question Answering in Context". In: *Proceedings of the 2018 Conference on Empirical Methods in Natural Language Processing (EMNLP)*. 2018, pp. 2174–2184.

[5] Philipp Christmann, Rishiraj Saha Roy, and Gerhard Weikum. "Explainable Conversational Question Answering over Heterogeneous Sources via Iterative Graph Neural Networks". In: *Proceedings of the 46th International ACM Conference on Research and Development in Information Retrieval (SIGIR)*. 2023, pp. 643–653.

[6] Wanyun Cui et al. "KBQA: Learning Question Answering over QA Corpora and Knowledge Bases". In: *In Proceedings of the VLDB Endowment* 10.5 (2017).

[7] Mauro De Gennaro, Eva G Krumhuber, and Gale Lucas. "Effectiveness of an Empathic Chatbot in Combating Adverse Effects of Social Exclusion on Mood". In: *Frontiers in Psychology* 10 (2020), p. 3061.

[8] Jianfeng Gao, Michel Galley, and Lihong Li. "Neural Approaches to Conversational AI". In: *Foundations and Trends in Information Retrieval* 13 (2019).

[9] Somil Gupta, Bhanu Pratap Singh Rawat, and Hong Yu. "Conversational Machine Comprehension: a Literature Review". In: *Proceedings of the 28th Interna-*

tional Conference on Computational Linguistics (COL-ING). 2020, pp. 2739–2753.

[10] Soyeong Jeong et al. "Phrase Retrieval for Open Domain Conversational Question Answering with Conversational Dependency Modeling via Contrastive Learning". In: *Findings of the Association for Computational Linguistics (ACL).* 2023, pp. 6019–6031.

[11] Mandar Joshi et al. "TriviaQA: A Large Scale Distantly Supervised Challenge Dataset for Reading Comprehension". In: *Proceedings of the 55th Annual Meeting of the Association for Computational Linguistics (ACL).* 2017, pp. 1601–1611.

[12] Vladimir Karpukhin et al. "Dense Passage Retrieval for Open-Domain Question Answering". In: *Proceedings of the 2020 Conference on Empirical Methods in Natural Language Processing (EMNLP).* 2020, pp. 6769–6781.

[13] Tomás Kociský et al. "The NarrativeQA Reading Comprehension Challenge". In: *Transactions of the Association for Computational Linguistics* (2018).

[14] Mike Lewis et al. "BART: Denoising Sequence-to-Sequence Pre-training for Natural Language Generation, Translation, and Comprehension". In: *Proceedings of the 58th Annual Meeting of the Association for Computational Linguistics (ACL).* 2020, pp. 7871–7880.

[15] Amit Mishra and Sanjay Kumar Jain. "A Survey on Question Answering Systems With Classification". In: *Journal of King Saud University-Computer and Information Sciences* 28.3 (2016).

[16] Minghui Qiu et al. "Reinforced History Backtracking for Conversational Question Answering". In: *Thirty-Fifth AAAI Conference on Artificial Intelligence (AAAI).* 2021, pp. 13718–13726.

[17] Chen Qu et al. "Attentive History Selection for Conversational Question Answering". In: *Proceedings of the 28th ACM International Conference on Information and Knowledge Management (CIKM).* 2019, pp. 1391–1400.

[18] Chen Qu et al. "BERT with History Answer Embedding for Conversational Question Answering". In: *Proceedings of the 42nd International ACM Conference on Research and Development in Information Retrieval (SIGIR).* 2019, pp. 1133–1136.

[19] Pranav Rajpurkar et al. "SQuAD: 100, 000+ Questions for Machine Comprehension of Text". In: *Proceedings of the Conference on Empirical Methods in Natural Language Processing (EMNLP).* 2016, pp. 2383–2392.

[20] Siva Reddy, Danqi Chen, and Christopher D. Manning. "CoQA: A Conversational Question Answering Challenge". In: *Transaction of Association for the Computational Linguistics* 7 (2019), pp. 1–8.

[21] Simon Suster and Walter Daelemans. "CliCR: a Dataset of Clinical Case Reports for Machine Reading Comprehension". In: *Proceedings of the 2018 Conference of the North American Chapter of the Association for Computational Linguistics: Human Language Technologies (NAACL-HLT).* 2018, pp. 1551–1563.

[22] Priyansh Trivedi et al. "LC-QuAD: A Corpus for Complex Question Answering over Knowledge Graphs". In: *Proceedings of the 16th International Semantic Web Conference (ISWC).* 2017, pp. 210–218.

[23] Joseph Weizenbaum. "ELIZA—A Computer Program For the Study of Natural Language Communication Between Man And Machine (Reprint)". In: *Communications of the ACM* 26.1 (1983).

[24] Munazza Zaib, Quan Z. Sheng, and Wei Emma Zhang. "A Short Survey of Pre-trained Language Models for Conversational AI-A New Age in NLP". In: *Proceedings of the Australasian Computer Science Week (ACSW)*. 2020, 11:1–11:4.

[25] Munazza Zaib et al. "BERT-CoQAC: BERT-based Conversational Question Answering in Context". In: *Proceeding of International Symposium on Parallel Architectures, Algorithms and Programming (PAAP)*. 2021, pp. 47–57.

[26] Munazza Zaib et al. "Conversational Question Answering: A Survey". In: *Knowledge and Information Systems* 64.12 (2022).

[27] Munazza Zaib et al. "Keeping the Questions Conversational: Using Structured Representations to Resolve Dependency in Conversational Question Answering". In: *International Joint Conference on Neural Networks (IJCNN)*. 2023, pp. 1–7.

[28] Munazza Zaib et al. "Learning Contrastive Representations for Dense Passage Retrieval in Open-domain Conversational Question Answering". In: *Proceedings of the 25th International Conference on Web Information Systems Engineering 2024 (WISE), under review.*

[29] Rowan Zellers et al. "SWAG: A Large-Scale Adversarial Dataset for Grounded Commonsense Inference". In: *Proceedings of the Conference on Empirical Methods in Natural Language Processing (EMNLP)*. 2018, pp. 93–104.

[30] Yongfeng Zhang et al. "Towards Conversational Search and Recommendation: System Ask, User Respond". In: *Proceedings of the 27th ACM International Conference on Information and Knowledge Management (CIKM)*. 2018, pp. 177–186.

CHAPTER 2

Role of Conversational Question Answering in Artificial Intelligence

This chapter provides a comprehensive review of the state-of-the-art works in the field of ConvQA (specifically CMRC), employing diverse techniques in their key components. Moreover, a detailed analysis of the ConvQA datasets comprising different characteristics has also been presented in addition to the discussion about the potential application of ConvQA in different avenues.

2.1 OVERVIEW

Challenges in ConvQA can be different depending on the underlying source they use for information retrieval, type of answer selection strategy employed (whether extractive or generative), and question's type [23]. This research work's primary focus is on text-based reading comprehension task with extractive answer span selection to multi-turn inter-connected questions. This chapter is an effort to provide a bird-eye overview of the state-of-the-art research trends of ConvQA primarily based on reviewed papers over recent

DOI: 10.1201/9781003592068-2

years. Our findings show that there has been a trend shift from single-turn to ConvQA which empowers the field of conversational search from different perspectives. Thus, the main contributions of this chapter can be listed as:

1. We deliberate the ConvQA paradigm and research trends pertinent to the same. We also describe the categorization of ConvQA at different levels.

2. Subsequently, we elaborate on the two broader categories of ConvQA, with a specific focus on "Conversational Machine Reading Comprehension (CMRC). We review the state-of-the-art in the field of CMRC with a focus on some key components, including but not limited to, the history selection module, encoder, reasoning module, and output predictor.

3. We review the characteristics and collection process of ConvQA-related datasets that have played an important role in advancing the said field.

4. We identify and subsequently discuss the practical applications of the subject domain.

The focus of this chapter is on understanding how the CMRC systems handle contextual nuances, adapt to multi-turn interactions, and leverage diverse information sources. As a whole, this chapter presents a comprehensive review of the advancements in ConvQA in the field of ConvAI and provides a way forward for future research directions.

2.1.1 Paper's Selection

The research papers reviewed in this chapter are high-quality papers selected from the top NLP and AI conferences, including but not limited to ACL[1], SIGIR[2],

---

[1]https://www.aclweb.org/
[2]https://sigir.org/

NeurIPS[3], NAACL[4], EMNLP[5], ICLR[6], AAAI[7], IJCAI[8], CIKM[9], SIGKDD[10], and WSDM[11]. Other than published research papers in the aforementioned conferences, we have also considered good papers in e-Print archive[12] as they manifest the latest research outputs. The papers are selected from the archive using three metrics: paper quality, method novelty, and the number of citations (optional). This chapter encompasses over 100 top-notch conferences and journal papers. The number of papers pertinent to ConvQA steadily increased from the year 2016 onwards, with the highest being in 2019. Coincidentally, 2019 also marks the year when the fields of natural language generation and natural language understanding were revolutionized with the introduction of pre-trained language models. These pre-trained language models have the potential to address the issue of data scarcity and bring considerable advantages by generating contextualized word embeddings [97]. This rise of interest depicts the gradual shift in focus of the researchers in both academia and industry in utilizing pre-trained language models for the design of ConvQA systems. We have reviewed papers from the top-conferences with ACL, SIGIR, and EMNLP being the top venues for natural language-related progress. It is noted, though, that more than 35% of the papers come from a variety of conferences/journals outside of the typical venues further attesting to the fact that this is an interdisciplinary topic spanning different areas such as knowledge management, knowledge discovery, and AI.

---

[3]https://nips.cc/
[4]https://naacl.org/
[5]https://sigdat.org/
[6]https://iclr.cc/
[7]https://www.aaai.org/
[8]https://www.ijcai.org/
[9]http://www.cikmconference.org/
[10]https://www.kdd.org/
[11]http://www.wsdm-conference.org/
[12]https://arxiv.org/

2. Foundations of QA and Introduction to ConvQA	3. Sequential KB-QA	4. CMRC	5. Datasets for ConvQA	6. Research Trends
➢ Categorization of ConvQA Systems ➢ Why ConvQA Differ from QA?	➢ Generic Architecture	➢ History Selection Module ➢ Encoder ➢ Reasoning Module ➢ Output Predictor	➢ CoQA ➢ QuAC ➢ OR-QuAC ➢ TopiOCQA	➢ Personal Assistants ➢ Customer Care ➢ Search Engines

FIGURE 2.1   Taxonomy of this chapter.

2.1.2   Chapter's Structure

The taxonomy of this chapter is shown in Figure. 2.1. In Section 2.2, we present a concise background on single-turn QA and introduce the discourse on ConvQA. This section also outlines the classification of ConvQA systems based on the sources they leverage to answer questions. Moving on to Section 2.3, a brief exploration of sequential KB-QA is provided, along with an overview of the components integrated into its generic architecture. Section 2.4 delves into the realm of CMRC. Our primary focus in this dissertation is CMRC, and we use the term ConvQA interchangeably to refer to this task. The section details how the general architecture of MRC can be adapted for CMRC, including the decomposition of the architecture into various modules and the techniques employed within each module. Section 2.5 outlines the datasets introduced to enhance advancements in ConvQA, accompanied by a qualitative comparison of each dataset. Section 2.6 underscores the potential applications of ConvQA systems in commercial domains and elucidates research trends that warrant exploration for more effective utilization of these systems. Finally, in Section 2.7, concluding remarks are offered.

2.2   FOUNDATIONS OF QA AND INTRODUCTION TO CONVQA

Question answering in general involves accessing different data sources to find the correct answer for an asked question, as depicted in Figure. 2.2. It dates back to the 1960s [50] when early QA systems, due to rule-based methods and absurdly small size of available datasets, did not achieve well, thereby making it difficult to be used in practical applications. These systems saw their rise in 2015 and this largely was associated with two driving factors:

(a) The use of deep learning methods to capture the critical information in QA tasks that outperform the traditional rule-based models.

(b) The availability of several large-scale datasets, i.e., Stanford Question Answering Dataset (SQuAD) [69], Freebase [6], Microsoft **MA**chine Reading **CO**mprehension (MS MARCO) [53], DBpedia [40], and CNN & DAILY MAIL [52], which make it possible to deal with the task of QA on neural architectures more efficiently and further provide a test bed for evaluating the performance of these models.

To realize the QA tasks more close to the real-world scenarios, several advanced research directions have emerged recently. One such direction is ConvQA [41], which introduces a new dimension of dialog systems that combines the elements of both chit-chat and QA. ConvQA is a *system ask, user respond* kind of setting where the system can ask a user multiple questions to understand the user's information need [98]. Usually, a user starts the conversation with a particular question in mind and the system searches its database to find an appropriate solution to that query. This could turn into a multi-turn conversation if the user needs to have more detailed information about the topic.

2.2.1   Categorization of ConvQA Systems

There are several ways of structuring the different aspects of a QA system. Since ConvQA is categorized as a sub-category of QA, the same categorization can be used for ConvQA systems as well. The categorization of the ConvQA model could

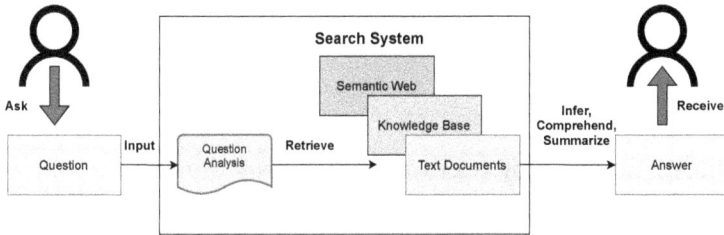

FIGURE 2.2   The high-level or generic architecture of QA systems where search system corresponds to the different sources. The specific architecture of a QA system depends on the underlying data source.

be realized on the basis of the data domain, types of questions, types of data sources, and the types of systems that we are building for the questions at hand [48]. Figure. 2.3 manifests the possible options that could be utilized to structure

Data Domains							
Open Domain QA				Closed Domain QA			
Wikipedia	DBPedia	Freebase	Web of Documents	Restaurant	Transport	Hotel	Movies

Types of Questions	
Factoid: (begins with 'wh' words) What/where/why	Casual: Why/How
Confirmation: (yes/no)	Listing Questions: (List the name of …)
Complex Questions: (requires inference and access to multiple documents)	Unanswerable Questions: (questions whose answers can not be inferred from given data source)

Types of Data Sources		
Structured	Semi-Structured	Unstructured
Databases, RDF Graphs	XML	Free-texts such as Wikipedia

Types of Systems	
Conversational Machine Reading Comprehension	Sequential KB-QA

FIGURE 2.3   Categorization of ConvQA based on: (i) data domains, (ii) types of questions, (iii) types of data sources, and (iv) types of systems [48].

a ConvQA system. The details of each of the categories are given in the rest of this section.

2.2.1.1 Data Domains

Questions asked by users are either open domain [31, 92] in which questions are domain-free and in a broad range, or restricted to specific application domains (i.e., closed domain) such as Travel [4], Restaurants [8], Movies [9], and Hospitals [8]. The question repository of a closed-domain question answering is smaller compared to open-domain question answering. This makes the models designed for closed-domain QA less transferable than the models for open-domain QA. It should be noted that the sub-categories of open-domain QA and closed-domain QA are examples of generic and task-specific datasets.

2.2.1.2 Types of Questions

Questions can be easily classified into various categories primarily depending upon their complexity, the nature of the response, or the techniques that should be utilized to answer them [48]. The classification based on the questions commonly asked by the users is delineated as follows:

Factoid Questions: Questions that expect the system to find a simple and fact-based answer in a short sentence, e.g., *"who acted as Chandler in FRIENDS?"*. Factoid questions typically begin with a *wh*-word. Different extraction techniques can be employed to find the answers to the factoid questions. The techniques first recover latent or hidden information in the given question, and then look for the answer in the given text using either structure matching [79] or reasoning [29]. FreebaseQA [31] is one of the examples of factoid QA dataset.

Confirmation Questions: Questions that require the answer in a binary format i.e., yes or no, e.g., *"Is Sydney the capital of Australia?"*. As the answers are not simple extractive text spans from the given source, a strong inference mechanism is needed to deduce the answers of confirmation type questions [48]. While there may be a lot of information given about a topic, analyzing if the original statement is true or not is still a challenging task.

Simple Questions: Simple questions require small piece of text to find an answer and, thus, they are easier to comprehend. For instance, for a question like *"What is the magnitude of earthquake in Pakistan?"*, it can easily be deduced that the answer of this question would be a simple numeric value. The process of finding an answer to a simple question consists of three basic steps: (i) question analysis, (ii) relevant documents/knowledge graphs retrieval, and (iii) answer extraction [7]. MS MARCO [53], SQuAD [69], and FreebaseQA [31] are some of the examples of simple questions-based datasets.

Complex Questions: Complex questions are questions that require different types of knowledge or several steps to answer. They are difficult to answer and require access to multiple documents or multiple interactions with the system [5]. Complex question like *"how many cities in China have more population than New Delhi?"* requires the system to first figure out the population of New Delhi and then compare it with the population of different cities in China. Thus, answering complex questions requires complex techniques such as iterative query generation [59], multi-hop reasoning [91], decomposition into sub-questions [28], and combining cues from the multiple documents [43]. Large-scale Complex Question Answering Dataset (LC-QuAD) [85] and Complex Sequential Question Answering (CSQA) [76] are some of the examples of complex QA datasets.

Casual Questions: Casual questions require detailed explanation pertinent to the entity and they usually start with the words like *why* or *how*. The answers generated for casual questions are not straight forward or concise. This generation of detailed answers call for advanced NLP techniques that are able to understand the question on different levels of technicality such as semantics and syntax [25]. An example of such questions could be *"why do earthquakes occur?"*.

Listing Questions: These are the questions that require the list of entities or facts as an answer, e.g., *"list the name of all the former presidents of America"*. The techniques that are utilized to answer factoid question works well for the listing questions.

The reason being that QA systems treat such questions as a sequence of factoid questions asked iteratively [48].

Unanswerable Questions: These are the questions whose answers cannot be found or deduced via the source text. Unanswerable questions could be any type of the aforementioned questions. For these questions, the correct result of the QA system is to indicate that it is unanswerable. SQuADRUn [68] is an extension of the SQuAD dataset [69] with over 50,000 unanswerable questions that was introduced to further improve the task of QA.

2.2.1.3 Types of Data Sources

ConvQA systems can be classified on the basis of the underlying data sources they utilize to find an answer. These underlying data sources could be:

Structured Data Source: In a structured document, data is stored in the form of entities. These entities form a separate table. An entity in a table can have multiple attributes associated with it. The definition of these attributes is referred to as the metadata and is stored in a schema. A query language is used to access the data and retrieve relevant information from the schema. Examples of structured data sources are databases and Resource Description Framework (RDF) graphs. Question Answering over Linked Data (QALD)[13] and LC-QuAD [85] utilize structured data source (i.e., RDF graphs) to answer the questions.

Semi-structured Data Source: There is no clearly defined boundary between the stored data and its schema in the semi-structured data sources, which makes it quite labor-intensive to build. An example of a semi-structured data source is XML. The datasets that are designed using semi-structured data sources, include TabMCQ [87] and Question Answering Using Semi-structured Metadata (QuaSM) [58].

Unstructured Data Source: There are no pre-defined rules for storing the data in this particular arrangement. The data stored in the unstructured data sources could be of any type and require the use of advanced NLP techniques and information retrieval methods to find out the relevant answer. However, the reliability of finding the correct answers is low as compared to the structured data sources. Examples of unstructured datasets are SQuAD [69], Question Answering in Context (QuAC) [12], and CNN & Daily Mail [24].

2.2.1.4 Types of ConvQA Systems

Over the past few years, the demand for ConvQA systems, from both research and commercial perspective, has increased in turn enabling users to search a large-scale knowledge-based (KB) or a text-based corpora written in natural language. This categorizes the ConvQA systems into sequential KB-QA agents and CMRC:

---

[13]http://qald.aksw.org/

Sequential KB-QA: KB-QA systems are extremely flexible and easy-to-use in contrast to the traditional SQL-based systems that require users to formulate complex SQL queries [14]. In a real-world scenario, users do not always ask simple questions [76]. Usually, the questions asked are complex in nature, and therefore, require multi-turn interaction with the KB. Also, once a question has been answered, the user tends to put forward another question that is linked to the previous question-answer pair. This forms the task of sequential QA using knowledge graphs.

Conversational Machine Reading Comprehension (CMRC): The practical use of text-based QA agents, also referred to as CMRC agents, is more common in the mobile phones than in the search engines (like Google, Bing, and Baidu), wherein concise and direct answers are provided to the users rather than presenting them with a list of possible answers. For instance, if a user intends to look for a popular restaurant in a particular geographical area, the search engine would provide her with a search result encompassing options spread on multiple pages, whereas, a CMRC-based dialog agent would ask a few follow-up questions to figure out the preference(s) of the user to subsequently narrow down the search result to one, i.e., possibly the best, answer. With the emergence of CMRC, many researchers [70, 12, 76, 28] have tried inducing a conversational aspect to meet the requirements for the task of ConvQA by introducing a background context and a series of inter-related questions.

2.2.2 What Makes ConvQA Different from QA?

2.2.2.1 Task-Based Differences

The task of ConvQA differs from the traditional QA in a number of ways. In traditional QA systems, questions are independent of each other and are based on the given passage. In contrast, questions in ConvQA are related to each other that poses an entirely different set of challenges including but not limited to:

- In order to find the correct answer for the question at hand, the model needs to encode not only the current question and source paragraph but also the previous history turns. More specifically, as shown in Table 2.1, Question 2 and Question 3 are related to Question 1.

- The turns in ConvQA are of a different nature. Some questions require more detailed information (i.e., *drilling down*), some may require information about some topic previously discussed (i.e., *topic shift*), some may ask about a topic again after it had been discussed (i.e., *topic return*), and some questions may ask for the clarification of topic (i.e., *clarification question*) [94]. All of these characteristics are incremental in nature and present challenges that most of the top-performing QA models fail to address directly, such as pragmatic reasoning and referring back to the previous context applying co-reference resolution. In Table 2.1, Question 2 is an example of a drill-down question, Question 3 is a clarification question, and *"it"* in Question 5 *"where is it?"* requires co-reference resolution.

2.2.2.2 Architectural Differences

The architecture of a ConvQA model is similar to the one of a QA system on the base level. However, to introduce the conversational touch to the system, a ConvQA model extends the traditional QA system by introducing a few modules. A ConvQA system differs from a traditional QA system in two aspects. First, the encoder is embedded with a sub-module referred to as the history modeling module responsible for not only encoding the current question and the given passage, but also the history turns of the conversation. Second,

TABLE 2.1   A Chunk of a Dialog from the CoQA Dataset [70].

Topic: Staten Island	
Passage:	Staten Island is one of the five boroughs of New York City in the U state of New York. In the southwest of the city, Staten Island is the southernmost part of both the city and state of New York, with Conference House Park at the southern tip of the island and the state. With a 2016 Census-estimated population of 476,015, Staten Island is the least populated of the boroughs but is the third-largest in area at. Staten Island is the only borough of New York with a non-Hispanic White majority. The borough is coextensive with Richmond County, and until 1975 was the Borough of Richmond. Its flag was later changed to reflect this. Staten Island has been sometimes called "the forgotten borough" by inhabitants who feel neglected by the city government.
Question 1:	How many burroughs are there?
Answer 1:	Five.
Question 2:	In what city?
Answer 2:	New York City.
Question 3:	And state?
Answer 3:	New York.
Question 4:	Is Staten Island one?
Answer 4:	Yes.
Question 5:	Where is it?
Answer 5:	In the southwest of the city
Question 6:	What is it sometimes called?
Answer 6:	The forgotten borough.

Co-references are highlighted in purple color and incomplete questions are shown in teal color.

a reasoning module is extended to generate an answer that might not be directly given in the passage, using pragmatic reasoning [70].

2.3 SEQUENTIAL KB-QA SYSTEMS

A KB is a structured information repository used for knowledge sharing and management purposes [44]. Freebase [6], NELL [49], DBpedia [40], and Wikidata[14] are well-known examples of large-scale graph-structured knowledge bases also termed as the Knowledge Graphs (KGs) and have become significant resources when dealing with open-domain questions. The KGs are known to be a graphical representation of a KB, and a typical KG comprises of triples encompassing subject, predicate, object triples *(s,r,t)*, wherein *r* is a relation or predicate between the entities *s* and *t* [21]. They play an important role in bridging up the lexical gap by providing additional information about relations which in turn helps in gaining more detailed information about the context. The knowledge graphs have seen their successful applications in various NLP tasks such as text entailment, information retrieval, and QA [100].

The task of QA over large-scale KB-QA systems has seen its progress from simple single-fact task to complex queries requiring multi-hop interaction and traversal of the knowledge graphs. These come under the category of single-turn QA where a user puts forward a question and the system finds the best possible answer for it. Though KB-QA-based agents improved the flexibility of QA process to a considerable extent, nevertheless, it is irrational to believe that these systems could constitute complex queries without having complete knowledge about the organizational structure of the KB to be questioned [22]. Thus, sequential KB-QA system is a more optimal option as it lets the users query the KB interactively.

The interactive sequential KB-QA system is useful in many commercial areas such as making a restaurant reservation [81], finding a hotel in a new city, finding a movie-on-demand [17], or asking for relevant information based on certain attributes. Figure. 2.4 illustrates how a sequential

---

[14]https://www.wikidata.org/wiki/Wikidata:Main_Page

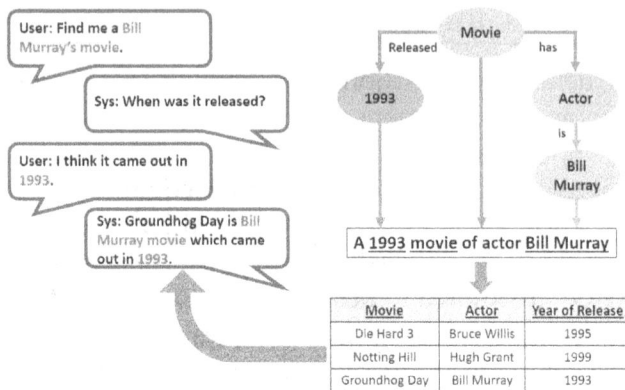

FIGURE 2.4 Aligning knowledge and conversation in sequential KB-QA.

KB-QA system aims to find a movie based on specified attributes by a user. If it is a traditional KB-QA system, the conversation would have ended after the first turn with a number of results. But under the sequential KB-QA setting, the system asks the follow-up questions for the specific details about the current question and present the user with the most appropriate answer.

Generic Architecture: The core architecture of a sequential KB-QA system comprises of a semantic parser and an inference engine, along with the addition of a dialog manager, that keeps track of the previous turns and decides which questions to ask to help the user query the KB effectively. The high-level architecture of a sequential KB-QA is depicted in Figure. 2.5, which consists of: (i) *Semantic Parser*, (ii) *Dialog Manager*, and (iii) *Response Generator*. The semantic parser is responsible for mapping input along with the previous context into a semantic representation (logical form) to query the KB. The dialog manager keeps track of the dialog history (i.e., QA pairs and DB state) and updates it accordingly [80].

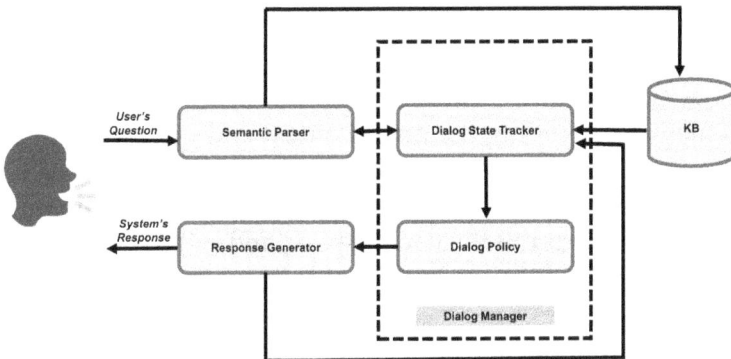

FIGURE 2.5   A high-level diagram of sequential KB-QA.

It is also responsible for selecting the system's next action (i.e., to provide an answer or to ask a clarification question) based on the current question using dialog policy. The process of dialog policy can be either trained on dialogs [89, 17] or programmed [90]. In the end, the response generator converts the system's action into natural language response. However, certain new approaches [51, 13] are working toward the elimination of the semantic parser module as it requires extensive and expensive labeling of data.

2.4   CONVERSATIONAL MACHINE READING COMPREHENSION

Most of the work carried out in the field of MRC is based on single-turn QA that is unlikely in the real-world scenario since humans tend to seek information in a conversational context [71]. For instance, a user might ask, "*Who is Christopher Columbus?*" and based on the answer received, he might further investigate, "*Where was he born?*" and "*What was he famous for?*". It is easy for a human to decipher that here "*he*" in the follow-up questions refer to "*Christopher Columbus*" from the first question. But when it comes to a machine to comprehend the context, it poses a set of challenges such as co-reference resolution or conversational history [41], which most of the state-of-the-art QA systems do not address directly.

A typical MRC model consists of three main functions namely: (i) encoding the given context and question into a set of symbolic representations called embeddings in a neural space, (ii) reasoning through the embeddings to find out the answer vector in the neural space, and (iii) decoding the answer vector to produce natural language output [21]. In [63], the authors proposed a modification by introducing two modules, i.e., history selection and history modeling modules to address the aforementioned challenges to incorporate the conversational aspect, hence introducing the task of CMRC.

Formally, given a context C, the conversation history in the form of question-answer pairs $Q_1, A_1; Q_2, A_2; ..., Q_{i-1}; A_{i-1}$, and a question Q_i, the CMRC model needs to predict the answer A_i. The answer A_i can either be a free-form text with evidence [70] or a text span [12]. The flow of a general CMRC model is depicted in Figure. 2.6.

These modules have been discussed separately in the rest of this section, along with the techniques and trends utilized in each of them for the successful design and implementation of a CMRC model.

2.4.1 History Selection Module

To enable the CMRC model to predict the answer span more accurately, it is necessary to introduce the previous context along with the source passage and current question. However, context utterances that are relevant to the query are useful, whereas irrelevant ones may bring more noise [83, 62]. Thus, the careful selection of conversational history turns is quite critical for the model. The history selection process can be categorized as:

Selecting K Turns: Contextual attention-based deep neural network (SDNet) [99], bidirectional attention flow

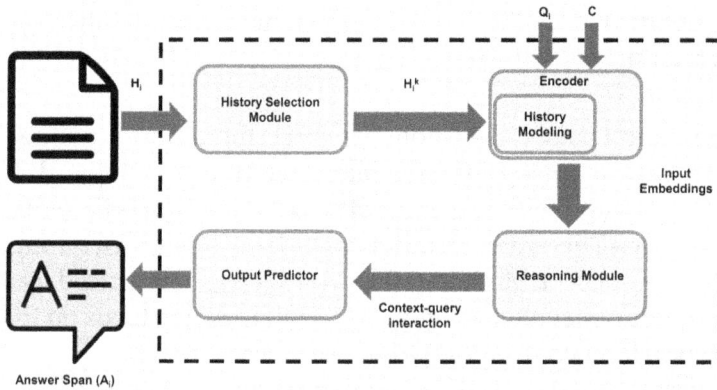

FIGURE 2.6 Generic framework of a CMRC model which consists of (i) history selection module that selects H_i' history turns from the conversational history context H_i; (ii) encoder that transforms the tokens of H_i', C, Q_i into input embeddings; (iii) reasoning module is responsible for performing contextual integration of input embeddings into contextualized embeddings to perform reasoning; and (iv) output predictor predicts the answer A_i on the basis of context-query interaction.

(BIDAF++) [12], open-retrieval ConvQA (ORConvQA) [64], and weakly supervised open-retrieval ConvQA (WS-OR-ConvQA) [65] utilize conversation history by incorporating K rounds of history turns.

Immediate History Turns: BERT with 2-ctx [54] suggests that incorporating immediate two turns can be helpful in predicting the right answer span, whereas BERT-HAE [63] (where BERT stand for Bidirectional Encoder Representations from Transformers and HAE stands for History Answer Embedding) claims that incorporating five to six conversational history turns contributes more in finding the correct answer span. However, both models demonstrate a dramatic degradation in the performance with the increase in the number of turns.

Dynamic History Selection: In [94], the authors pointed out that the dialog features like topic return or topic shift may not align with the concept of selecting immediate dialog turns. Therefore, in order to address this shortcoming, History Answer Modeling (HAM) [62] was introduced as a dynamic policy that weighs the previous dialog turns on the basis of their contribution to answering the current question. The model assigns weight by attending the previous history turns at a token level or sentence level and combine the same with the current turn's representation.

Another approach, referred to as Env-ConvQA [60], proposed a dynamic k-history turns selection process based on reward-based reinforced backtracking policy. The model treats the process of extracting the relevant history turns as a sequential decision-making process. The model acts on the provided turns and backtracks through each turn one by one to decide whether the turn is relevant to the current question or not.

2.4.2 Encoder

This component is responsible for converting the tokens of the source passage, current question, and the selected history turns into fixed-length vectors which are subsequently provided as an input to the reasoning module. Although the internals of an encoder may vary from approach to approach depending on the input required by the reasoning module, nevertheless, the high-level encoding generally involves transforming and combining different context-dependent word embeddings, including but not limited to, Embeddings from Language Model (ELMo) [57], GloVE [56], and BERT [16]. To improve the impact of these embeddings, additional features such as Parts of Speech (POS) tags and HAE have also been incorporated as a part of the input. These embeddings can be categorized into conventional word embeddings and contextualized word embeddings.

Conventional Word Embeddings: This technique is responsible for encoding of words into low-dimensional vectors. The encoding is done in such a way that the inter-related tokens are placed in close proximity to each other in vector space to make the identification of co-relation easy between them. Several methods for generating distributed word representation have been proposed in the literature, with the most popular and efficient being GloVE [56] and Word2Vec [46]. However, these methods fail to determine the accurate meaning of the words with respect to their given context.

Pre-trained Contextualized Word Embeddings: Though the conventional word embeddings method yields good results in identifying and establishing the correlation between the words encoded in low-dimensional vectors, they still fail to capture the contextual representations sufficiently. To be accurate, the distributed word representations generated for a single word are the same in varying contexts. To overcome this issue, the idea of contextualized embeddings was put forward by the researchers. These embeddings are pre-trained on large corpora of text and are then utilized as either distributed word embeddings or are fine-tuned according to the specific downstream task. This comes under the category of transfer learning and has obtained astonishing results in various NLP-based tasks [16, 57, 93].

The most successful application of these embeddings has been in the field of machine comprehension. One of the very first in the series is Context Vectors (CoVe) [45] that utilizes Seq2Seq models [82] to train Long Short-Term Memory (LSTM) [26] encoders on a large-scale dataset. The encoder then utilizes the obtained results on other downstream NLP tasks. Proposed by [57], ELMo is a successor of CoVe and embeddings are obtained by training a bi-directional

Language Model (biLM). These embeddings can generate more accurate representations of the words as instead of using the results from the topmost layer of biLM, it combine outcomes from all the layers of biLM into one vector and assign a weighting score that is task-specific.

Another popular model in terms of language understanding is Transformer [86] which is a sequence transduction model based on multi-headed attention, thus eliminating the need to utilize multiple recurrent layers that are part of most encoder-decoder architectures. This mechanism of self-attention makes the transformer more efficient and parallelizable in learning the context of the input sequences. The most popular and top-trending one in the series is BERT [16], which has addressed the issue of unidirectionality used in training of different language models such as Generative Pre-training (GPT) [66] and GPT-2 [67]. Due to the bi-directional property and the powerful transformer [86] architecture, BERT's performance exceeds the top-performing models in many NLP downstream tasks [16]. Within no time, numerous models are derived from BERT, such as SpanBERT [32], which masks spans instead of tokens; ALBERT [39], which is smaller and faster to train; RoBERTa [42], which trains for longer with a more varied masking pattern; and XLNet [93] and Transformer-XL [15], which use an autoregressive pre-training approach to better handle long-distance dependencies. A complete taxonomy of BERT-derived models can be found in [73] and [61].

2.4.3 History Modeling

The process of history modeling is generally carried out in the encoder module, where the conversation history is integrated with the context and current question to form a complete input. We describe it as a separate module for easy understanding and better readability. Different models employ different techniques or a combination of these to introduce conversational history turns as a part of an input.

A brief description of each of these techniques is given as follows:

Appending the Conversation History: One of the most common ways to include the selected history turns (previous question answer pairs) as a part of the input is by appending them with the current question [64, 99, 60] . This is further modified at sublevel by some approaches [11, 54] via appending only history questions along with the turn number encoded with it. In [12], the authors claimed that adding dialog turn in the input yields better results practically.

Introducing History Answer Markers in the Given Context: Another trend seen recently in modeling the conversation history is encoding the context tokens in history answer embeddings markers [63]. The advantage of using these tokens is that they work as an indicator to point out whether a context token is a part of history answer or not. Another variation of HAE is Positional HAE (POS-HAE) [62], wherein position information of dialog turn relative to the current question is also encoded. This enables the model to capture the spatial patterns of history answers in context.

Generating Latent Representations Using Context Tokens: One of the attributes of successful CMRC models is being able to grasp the flow of the conversation. Since the flow of the conversation is based on the context, it can be captured by generating latent or intermediate representations of the context tokens rather than using the raw inputs. Such approaches [27, 95] fall under the category of flow-based methods.

2.4.4 Reasoning Module

CMRC models can be grouped based on how they perform the process of reasoning. For *single-step reasoning*, the model passes the contextualized input (context, question, and history turns) only across one layer and generates the answer. In contrast, for *multi-step reasoning*, the contextualized input is fused across multiple layers to produce history-aware contextualized output embeddings. Generally, the input for this module consists of multiple sequence sets which are then fused in multiple layers and are usually interwined with an attention mechanism to generate accurate output embeddings. On the basis of underlying techniques, the reasoning process can be categorized as *conventional methods, pretrained language models, flow-based models,* and *open-retrieval based models.*

2.4.4.1 Conventional Methods

Several sequence models employing different mechanisms like self-attention and bidirectional attention are a common choice for carrying out the task of CMRC. Famous as CoQA's baseline, DrQA+PGNet [70] leverages the strengths of two powerful models, i.e., Pointer-Generator Network (PGNet) [77] and Document Reader (DrQA) [10]. DrQA, based on bi-directional LSTM (biLSTM), first provides cues from the answer evidence in the given context. PGNet, which utilizes an attention-based Seq2Seq model [3], decodes the found evidence to predict the final answer.

BiDAF++ [12] uses the bi-directional Attention Flow (BiDAF) [78] model augmenting the bi-directional attention flow along with contextualized embeddings and self-attention. The modeling performs reasoning via a multi-layered bidirectional attention flow layer followed by a multi-layered biLSTM to identify the correct answer span. SDNet [99] utilizes two bidirectional Recurrent Neural Networks (RNNs) [74] to apply both self-attention and inter-attention between different layers in order to form the contextualized understanding of question and context.

2.4.4.2 Pre-trained Language Models

Large-scale pre-trained language models such as BERT [16], RoBERTa [42], and GPT [66] have become popular to achieve the state-of-the-art results on NLP tasks. While GPT is known for its language generation capabilities, BERT is famous for language understanding and has provided great results in machine comprehension tasks. One of the advantages of employing pre-trained language models is their capability to fuse both encoding and reasoning modules together. This results in a ready-to-tune architecture that hides the complex interactional nature between the given context and current question. However, incorporating previous context is a challenging task in pre-trained language models (particularly BERT) as it allows for only two segments in the input and the length of sequence is limited to 512. The more turns we try to append, the more context paragraph or history turns need to be truncated to be able to adapt to the model. The accurate modeling of the history results in better reasoning over the context. The history integration challenge can be addressed using the following approaches:

- Highlighting conversational history by embedding history answer embeddings in the contextual tokens as suggested in BERT-HAE [62]. The embeddings are only added for those tokens that are present in the previous conversational history.

- Using separate models for all the history turns to attend to the interaction between each turn and the given context as suggested by Ohsugi et al. [54]. The contextualized embeddings are then merged together to form an aggregated history-aware embeddings. These aggregated embeddings are then passed from BiGRU to capture an inter-turn interaction before any prediction can be made.

- Introducing a reinforced backtracker in the model to filter out the unnecessary or irrelevant history turns instead of evaluating them as a whole as proposed by Qiu et al. [60]. The selected turns along with the given passage forms an input to be provided to the BERT model.

Once the history turns have been integrated, BERT-based models calculate the probability of each word being the start word by generating a dot product between the final embedding and the start vector, followed by the application of softmax over all the words [63]. Finally, the word with the highest probability value is selected. A similar process is employed to locate the final word in the given context. In [60], the model after predicting the answer span generates a reward to evaluate the utility of the history selection for answer prediction process. The computed reward, in turn, is utilized to update the policy network to maximize the accuracy of the model for the next cycle of prediction.

2.4.4.3 Flow-Based Models

Another recent trend that has caught attention is the use of flow-based approaches in machine comprehension. A well-designed CMRC model should be able to grasp the flow of the conversation, i.e., knowing what topic is under discussion as well as facts and events relevant to it. Thus, the flow of conversation can be considered as a sequence of latent representations generated based on the token of source passage. These latent representations, generated during the reasoning of previous conversations, aid in the contextual reasoning of the question. The main models based on flow architecture are described as:

FlowQA [27] utilizes the contextualized embeddings as the latent representations, a process often referred to as Integration Flow (IF). The process involves the sequential processing of the context tokens in parallel to the question turns (referred to as context integration) along with processing question turns sequentially parallel to context tokens (flow).

The model utilizes multiple flow layers interweaved with attention first on the context and then on the question itself to come up with the reasoning for the answer.

FlowDelta [95] was introduced as an improved version in the flow series that utilizes the same architecture as FlowQA but achieves better accuracy. Instead of using the intermediate or latent representations, the model passes the information gain through the reasoning process. The information gain is nothing but the difference between the latent representations of the previous two layers. By modeling such difference, the model would better focus on the information hints present in the context.

The previously discussed flow approaches follow the concept of IF that does not really mimic a human's style of reasoning. The underlying reason is that they first perform reasoning in parallel for each question and then refine and enhance the reasoning across different turns. Graph Flow [11], on the other hand, constructs a dynamic context graph encoding not only the passage itself but also the question as well as the conversation history. The model processes the flow by applying GNN on all the sequences of context graphs and the output is utilized when processing the next graph. To capture the contextual relationship between the words, a biLSTM is applied before providing the words as an input to GNN. The Graph Flow architecture alternates this mechanism with co-attention over the question and the GNN output.

2.4.4.4 Open-Domain Conversational Question Answering Based Models

Another recently introduced trend in the field of CMRC is the use of open-domain retrieval methods. The methods discussed above rely heavily on the given passage to extract or generate an answer. However, this seems impractical in real-world scenarios since the availability of gold passage is not always possible. Thus, the model should be able to

retrieve the relevant passages from a collection. The main models employing the open-retrieval architecture are discussed
below:

OR-ConvQA [64] is first in the series of open-domain retrieval models for CMRC. It consists of three main modules: (i) a passage retriever, (ii) a re-ranker, and (iii) a passage reader. The three modules are based on Transformers [86]. The passage retriever first extracts the top-K relevant paragraphs from a collection provided a current question and the previous history. The retriever is based on dual-encoder architecture that utilizes two separate ALBERT [39] encoders for passages and questions. The re-ranker and reader uses the same BERT encoder. The encoder transforms the input sequence consisting of question, history, and relevant passages into the contextualized representations to be utilized by re-ranker and reader for answer extraction. The re-ranker module conducts a list-wise re-ranking of the retrieved passages that serves as a supervision signal to fine-tune the encoder. In the end, the answer span is predicted by the reader module by computing the probability of the tokens being a start/end token.

In OD-ConvQA, the model focuses on identifying and extracting short-span based answers. In information-seeking dialog, however, answers are relatively free-form and long which are difficult to extract. WS-ORConvQA [65] is an extension of ORConvQA and introduces a learned weak supervision approach that can find and extract both span-based and free-form answers. If the exact match is not found, the model tries to find a span in the retrieved passages that has the maximum overlap with the gold answer. Given a question and its conversation history, the passage retriever first extracts the relevant paragraphs from a collection. The retriever assigns a score based on the dot product of the representations of the questions and the passage. The reader then reads the top passages and produces an answer. The model works on a weakly supervised training approach. Given one of the retrieved passages and a gold answer, the weak supervisor predicts a span in the passage as a weak answer to provide weak supervision signals for training the reader. The reader is based on the standard BERT-based machine comprehension model [16] that calculates the probability of tokens being a start and an end token. The final answer is selected by computing the sum of its retriever score and reader score. Another recent work [2] highlighted the need to resolve co-references and ellipsis on OD-ConvQA to better understand the question. To resolve conversational dependencies, the approach suggests re-writing the question from scratch to better understand the context.

Another new trend within the field of OD-ConvQA is the utilization of DPR techniques [35, 34, 96]. A potential system approach involves initially encoding each conversational query into an embedding that effectively captures the user's information requirements. Subsequently, this encoded representation can be directly matched with documents within the learned embedding space. The utilization of denser retrieval in conversational search is particularly interesting. Conversational search endeavors to model the user's information needs based on ongoing conversation contexts, presenting a more pronounced vocabulary mismatch challenge. This is precisely the scenario where denser retrieval excels in ad hoc search. A recent study by Jeong et al. [30] concentrated on DPR through contrastive learning. Their model omits the reader module and directly predicts answer phrases in the retrieval module. Additionally, Fang et al. [20] introduced ConvADR-QA, emphasizing the importance of incorporating historical answers into the model as input and examining its influence on the overall model performance.

2.4.5 Output Prediction

The common trends that have been observed for the answer prediction module include span prediction, free-form answer prediction, and dialog acts prediction. For span prediction, the probabilities of tokens being the end and start token are calculated. For unanswerable questions, a token, UNANSWERED, is appended at the end of each passage in QuAC. The model learns to predict this token if it finds the question unanswerable. A sequence-level aggregated representation is used to calculate dialog-act prediction and the modeling of history dialog acts is not required for the prediction of this task. One recent work [30], in the field of OD-ConvQA, has suggested phrase retrieval to avoid the issue of error propagation. The model omits the reader module and utilizes a retriever only to retrieve the passages. The categorization of the architecture based on the techniques used in each module is summarized in Table 2.2.

2.5 DATASETS FOR CONVERSATIONAL QUESTION ANSWERING

One driver for the rapid growth in the field of ConvQA is the emergence of large-scale conversational datasets for both knowledge-base and machine comprehension. Constructing a high-quality dataset is equally significant as optimizing ConvQA-based architectures. In this section, we collect and compare the major datasets in the area of ConvQA. Generally, the datasets for machine reading comprehension fall into three categories based on the type of answer they provide:

- *Multiple-choice option* datasets provide text-based multiple choice question and expect the model to identify the right answer out of the available options. The examples of such datasets include the ReAding Comprehension Dataset from Examinations (RACE) [38], Machine Comprehension Text (MCTest) [72], and MCScript [55].

TABLE 2.2   Recent Studies on Conversational Machine Reading Comprehension (2016–2023).

Ref.	History Selection	Encoder	History Modeling	Reasoning	Output Prediction
			Traditional Models		
[12]	*k* history turns.	- GloVE for word embeddings. - BiDirectional LSTM for contextual embeddings.	- Encodes context tokens with history answer markers before passing on for reasoning. - Encode dialog turn number within the question embeddings.	Performs reasoning via multi-layered bidirectional attention flow layer followed by multi-layered biLSTM.	Span prediction.
[70]	*k* history turns.	Bidirectional LSTM.	- Appends the selected history turns to the source passage and current question.	DrQA model first point toward the evidence in the given text, PGNet then transform the evidence into the answer.	Free-form answers.
[99]	*k* history turns.	- Word embeddings using GloVe. - Contextualized embeddings using BERT.	- Appends the selected history turns to the source passage and current question.	Utilizes both self-attention and inter attention in multiple layers using biDirectional LSTM to reason across the given context.	Span prediction.
			BERT-based Models		

Continued on next page

TABLE 2.2 – continued from previous page

Ref.	History Selection	Encoder	History Modeling	Reasoning	Output Prediction
[63]	k history turns but found the optimal answer in five and six history turns.	BERT-generated embeddings.	- Introduce history answer marker layer to the context token is present in any conversational history answer or not.	- BERT generates a representation for each token based on the embeddings for position, segment, and tokens. - The model then computes the probability of tokens in a given paragraph of being a start and end token of the answer span.	Span prediction.
[62]	Dynamic history selection policy.	Bert-based embeddings on both word and sequence level.	- Encode context tokens with dialog-turn encoded variant of HAE called *POS HAE*.	History attention module assigns weight to each token-level and sequence-level representation. And then aggregated representations of both are obtained that are further used for answer prediction.	- Span prediction. - Dialog-act prediction.
[54]	k history turns.	Contextualized paragraph representations independently conditioned with each question and each answer generated using BERT.	- Appends history QA pair to the current question with each QA pair conditioned on the source paragraph. - The model then concatenates the resulting sequences to form a uniform representation.	The concatenated result is then passed through the BiGRU for span prediction.	- Span prediction. - Answer type prediction. (yes, no, unanswerable).

Continued on next page

TABLE 2.2 – continued from previous page

Ref.	History Selection	Encoder	History Modeling	Reasoning	Output Prediction
[60]	Dynamic k history turns.	BERT-generated embeddings.	- Prepends selected subset of history QA pair and passage to the current question. - The model then concatenates the resulting sequences to form a uniform representation.	- BERT generates a representation for each token based on the embeddings for position, segment, and tokens. - The model then computes the probability of tokens in a given paragraph of being a start and end token of the answer span. - After answer prediction, the model generates a reward to evaluate the role of selected history turns and update the policy network accordingly.	Span prediction.
			Flow-based Models		
[27]	k history turns.	Uses ELMo to generate contextual embeddings before passing it to IF layer.	Integrates both QA pairs and the intermediate context representation from conversation history called **FLOW**.	Employ multiple integration flow layers with alternating cross and self-attention to perform reasoning.	Span prediction.
[11]	Prepends N question answer pairs to the current question.	GloVE and 1024-dim BERT embeddings.	Encodes history QA pairs into contextual graphs.	BiLSTM is utilized for the context integration and the GNNs are used to capture the contextual interaction.	Span prediction.

Continued on next page

TABLE 2.2 – continued from previous page

Ref.	History Selection	Encoder	History Modeling	Reasoning	Output Prediction
[95]	k history turns.	Uses ELMo to generate contextual embeddings before passing it to IF layer.	Integrates both QA pairs and the intermediate context representation from conversation history called **FLOW**.	Model passes the information gain (the difference between the latent representations of last two layers) to let the model focus more precisely on the context.	Span prediction.
			OD-ConvQA Models		
[64]	k history turns.	Uses ALBERT to generate contextual embeddings before passing it to reader and reranker modules.	- Appends history questions to the current question. - The model uses two encoders, one for encoding current question with its history and other for encoding relevant passages.	- Employs fully supervised setting for the training of the reader. - The top-retrieved passages are then fed to the reranker and reader for a concurrent learning of all model components. - The reader predicts an answer by computing scores of each token being the start token and the end token.	Span prediction.

Continued on next page

TABLE 2.2 – continued from previous page

Ref.	History Selection	Encoder	History Modeling	Reasoning	Output Prediction
[65]	k history turns.	Uses ALBERT to generate contextual embeddings before passing it to reader module.	- Appends history questions to the current question. - The model uses two encoders, one for encoding current question with its history and other for encoding relevant passages. - The retriever generates a score based on the dot product of the representations of the question and the passage.	- Employs weakly supervised setting for the training of the reader. - The top-retrieved passages are then fed to the reader. - The reader computes the probabilities of the true start and end tokens among all the tokens from the top passages. - The answer span is selected on the basis of the sum of the retriever score and reader score.	- Span prediction. - Free-form answer.
[30]	k history turns.	Uses DPR to jointly encode the question and the conversational context.	- Appends the k conversational turns. - The model uses two encoders, one for encoding current question with its history and other for encoding relevant passages. - The retriever generates a score based on the dot product of the representations of the question and the passage.	- Skips the reader modules. - Uses contrastive learning to identify the similar turns in a dialog. - The words in the passages are pre-indexed. - The goal is to find only the locations of the answer based on its similarity to the input context.	- Phrase generation. - Free-form answer.

Continued on next page

TABLE 2.2 – continued from previous page

Ref.	History Selection	Encoder	History Modeling	Reasoning	Output Prediction
[20]	k history answers.	Uses dual-encoder architecture to map passages and the question.	- Appends k historical answers. - The input of the question encoder is the concatenation of the current question and k historical answers. - The retriever generates a score based on the dot product of the representations of the question and the passage.	- The reader first extracts a span for each passage by choosing the highest score of start and end tokens. - The final answer is obtained by multiplying the retriever score and the sum of start/end token score as the reader score.	Span extraction.

- *Descriptive answer* datasets allow answers to be in any free-form text. Such datasets are useful in situations, wherein the questions are implicit and may require the use of common sense or world knowledge. The examples include MS MARCO [53] and Narrative QA [36].

- *Span prediction* or *extractive* datasets require the model to extract the correct answer span from the given source passage. Such datasets provide better natural language understandability and easy evaluation of the task. SQuAD [69], TriviaQA [33], and NewsQA [84] are some popular examples of extractive datasets.

CoQA [70] and QuAC [12] are the two datasets for ConvQA, whereas OD-CONVQA is supported by OR-QuAC [64] and TopiOCQA [1]. These datasets come under the category of span-prediction. Apart from these two datasets, there is another ConvQA dataset, ShARC [75], which requires the understanding of a rule-text to answer a few inter-linked and co-referenced questions. These generated questions need to be answered using reasoning on the basis of background knowledge. However, this dataset does not really follow the definition of CMRC and is hence ignored. A summarized comparison pertaining to significant characteristics of both ConvQA and OD-COnvQA are presented in Table 2.3 and Table 2.4, respectively.

2.5.1   CoQA

CoQA was introduced by Reddy et al. [70] to measure a machine's ability to participate in a QA style conversation. The dataset was developed with three objectives in mind. The first is the nature of questions in human conversations. In this dataset, every question except the first one is dependent on the conversation history to make it more similar to the real-life setting of human conversation. The second goal of CoQA is to maintain the naturalness of answers in a

TABLE 2.3   A Comparison of the Multi-turn Conversational Datasets—CoQA [70] and QuAC [12] Based on Different Characteristics as Defined in Their Respective Papers

Characteristics	CoQA	QuAC
Data source	Passages collected from seven diverse domains, e.g., children's stories (MCTest), news articles (CNN), Wikipedia articles, etc.	Sections from Wikipedia articles filtered in the "people" category associated with subcategories like culture, animals, geography, etc.
Conversational setup	Questioner-answerer setting where both have access to the full context.	Teacher-student setup: the teacher has full context; the student only sees the title and summary.
Requires external Knowledge?	Yes.	No
Question type	Factoid.	Open-ended, highly contextual
Answer type	Free-form with an extractive rationale.	Extractive span, may include yes/no or "No Answer".
Dialog acts	No.	Yes.
Max turns per dialog	15.	11.
Unanswerable questions	Yes.	Yes.
Total number of questions	126K.	100K.
Total number of dialogs	8K.	14K.

conversation. Many existing datasets limit answers to be found in the given source passage. However, such a setting does not always ensure natural answers. In CoQA, the authors address this issue by proposing free-form answers while providing a text-span from the given passage as a rationale to the answer.

The third goal of CoQA is to facilitate the development of ConvQA systems across multiple domains. The existing QA datasets mainly focus on a single domain that results in complications to test the generalization capabilities of the existing systems. Thus, CoQA extends its domains, i.e., each with its own data source. These domains include articles based on literature extracted from Project Gutenberg,[15] children's stories taken from MCTest [72], Wikipedia articles,[16] Reddit articles from Writing Prompt [19], middle and high school English exams taken from [38], science articles derived from Ai2 science question [88], and news articles taken

---

[15]https://www.gutenberg.org/
[16]https://www.wikipedia.org/

TABLE 2.4 A Comparison of the OD-ConvQA Dataset—OR-QuAC [64] and TopiOCQA [1] Based on Different Characteristics as Defined in Their Respective papers

Characteristics	OR-QuAC	TopiOCQA
Data source	Collected by extending and combining QuAC, CANARD, and Wikipedia corpus.	Sections from Wikipedia articles filtered in the "people" category associated with subcategories like culture, animals, geography, etc.
Conversational setup	Real human-human dialogs between an information seeker and provider. The seeker learns about a hidden Wikipedia passage by asking free-form questions, having access only to the title and summary.	Each conversation is an interaction between two annotators—a questioner and an answerer.
Information-seeking?	Yes.	Yes.
Question type	Factoid.	Open-ended, highly contextual.
Answer type	Extractive span (including yes/no or 'No Answer').	Free-form with an extractive rationale.
Free-form Answers?	No.	Yes.
Max turns per dialog	11.	13.
Total number of dialogs	8K.	14K.

from CNN [24]. Evaluation and Reddit are used for out-of-domain evaluation only.

Data Collection: Each conversation is prepared in a two annotator setting, i.e., one being a questioner and the other being an answerer. The platform of Amazon Mechanical Turk (AMT)[17] is used to pair workers on a passage through the ParlAI MTurk API [47] and both the annotators have full access to the passage.

Dataset Analysis: The dataset consists of 127K conversation turns gathered from 8K conversations over text passages. The average length of a conversation is 15 turns and each turn consists of a question and an answer. The distribution of CoQA is spread across multiple question types. Prefixes like *did, where, was, is,* and *does* are very frequent in the dataset. Also, almost every sector of CoQA contains co-references which shows that it is highly conversational. What makes conversations in CoQA even more human-like

---

[17]https://www.mturk.com/

is that sometimes they just feature one-word questions like "Who?" or "Where?" or even "Why?". This shows that questions are context-dependent, and in order to answer correctly, the system needs to go through the previous history turns to understand the question.

Evaluation: The main evaluation metric for the dataset is macro-average F1 score of word overlap and is computed separately for in-domain and out-of-domain as well.

2.5.2 QuAC

In an information-seeking dialog, the students keep asking their teacher questions for clarification about a particular topic. This idea forms the basis for this newly introduced dataset, QuAC [12]. Modeling such inter-related questions can be complex as the questions can be elliptical, highly context-dependent, and even sometimes unanswerable. To promote learning in such a challenging situation, QuAC presents a rich set of 14K crowd-sourced QA dialogs (consisting of 100K QA pairs).

Dataset Collection: The nature of interaction in QuAC is of student-teacher where the teacher has the access to the source paragraph. A student only provided with the heading of the paragraph aims to gain as much knowledge about its content as possible by asking multiple questions. The teacher tries to answer the questions by extracting correct answer spans from the source passage. Also, the teacher uses dialog acts as feedback to the students (i.e., may or may not ask a follow-up question) which results in more productive dialogs.

Dataset Analysis: The dataset has long answers of maximum of 15 tokens which is an improvement over SQuAD and CoQA. Another factor worth noting is that frequent question types in QuAC are based on *Wh* words that make the questions more open-ended, in contrast to the other QA datasets where questions are more factoid. Furthermore, 86% of the questions are highly contextual, i.e., they require the model to re-read the context to resolve the co-references. Out of these questions, 44% refer to entities or events in the dialog history, whereas 61% refer to the subject of the article.

Evaluation: Besides evaluating the accuracy using the F1 score, QuAC also utilizes human equivalence score (HEQ) to measure a system's performance by finding the percentage of exceeding or matching an average human's performance. HEQ-Q and HEQ-D are, therefore, HEQ scores with the instances as questions and dialogs, respectively.

2.5.3   OR-QuAC

The OR-QuAC [64] dataset improves upon QuAC by adapting it to an open-retrieval setting. It is a composite dataset derived from three existing datasets: (1) the QuAC dataset [12], which provides information-seeking conversations, (2) the CANARD dataset [18], consisting of context-independent rewrites of QuAC questions, and (3) the Wikipedia corpus, serving as the knowledge source for answering questions.

Dataset Collection: The entire Wikipedia corpus is utilized to create a collection of passages for the OR-QuAC dataset, given that QuAC passages are sourced from Wikipedia. The English Wikipedia dump from October 20, 2019 is used for this purpose. The Wikipedia passages in QuAC are obtained through PetScan, and due to the unavailability of the exact date of the data dump, the latest dump is employed instead of trying to match the date of QuAC. The WikiExtractor is then applied to extract and clean text from the data dump, resulting in over 5.9 million Wikipedia articles. These articles are subsequently split into chunks with a maximum of 384 word pieces using the BERT tokenizer. The greedy split is performed while preserving sentence boundaries, and these chunks are referred to as passages.

To make the passages suitable for transformer-based retrievers and readers, the split is conducted with less than 0.5% of known answers being split into different passages. Questions corresponding to these split answers are considered unanswerable during training. The choice of passage-level retrieval over article-level retrieval is influenced by the belief that a full article may contain non-relevant content, and a sentence may lack context information. The split process is repeated for QuAC paragraphs, and Wikipedia passages are replaced with QuAC passages that share the same article titles. The positions of the ground truth answer spans are mapped to the new passages. The resulting collection comprises over 11 million passages for retrieval.

Dataset Analysis: The dataset has an average question length of 6.7 tokens and an average answer length of 12.5 tokens. Each dialog comprises 11 turns. The dataset includes 35,526 conversational turns for training, 3,430 for validation, and 5,571 for testing.

Evaluation: The QuAC challenge employs two crucial metrics, Word-level F1 and the human equivalence score (HEQ), to evaluate Conversational Question Answering (ConvQA) systems. Word-level F1 assesses the overlap between the predicted answer span and the ground truth answer span, serving as the primary metric for evaluating the overall system performance. HEQ measures the percentage of examples for which the system's F1 exceeds or matches the human F1, evaluating whether a system can provide answers as good as an average human. HEQ is computed at both the question level (HEQ-Q) and the dialog level (HEQ-D).

In addition to F1 and HEQ, Mean Reciprocal Rank (MRR) and Recall are utilized to evaluate the retrieval performance for both the retriever and reranker components. MRR reflects how well these components contribute to the overall score, computed as the mean of the reciprocal ranks of all queries. Recall measures the fraction of the total relevant passages that are retrieved. Recall is computed for the retriever only, as reranking does not impact this measure. This metric assesses whether the retriever can provide reasonable retrieval performance for the rest of the system. All retrieval metrics are calculated for the top five passages retrieved for the reader/reranker.

2.5.4 TopiOCQA

TopiOCQA [1], which stands for Topic Switching in Open-Domain Conversational Question Answering, is a large-scale dataset designed for information-seeking conversations in an open domain based on the Wikipedia corpus. Each Wikipedia document is treated as a separate topic in this dataset. Conversations in TopiOCQA start with a real information-seeking question from Natural Questions [37] to establish a seed topic (document). Subsequently, the questioner may shift to other related topics (documents) as the conversation progresses.

Dataset Collection: In TopiOCQA, every interaction involves two annotators—an individual posing questions and another providing answers. Throughout the conversation, the questioner is deliberately not shown the content of the documents, except for the main title and section titles. This setup simulates an information-seeking scenario, while the answerer has full access to the content along with the hyperlink structure for navigation. In each turn, both the questioner and answerer use free-form text for conversation in contrast to the extractive text spans commonly used for answerers in many existing datasets.

Dataset Analysis: Three thousand nine hundred twenty conversations, comprising 50,466 turns, were gathered.

Annotators were prompted to complete a minimum of ten turns, and conversations with fewer than five turns were excluded. The data was then divided into train, development, and test splits. Typically, a conversation in TopiOCQA comprises an average of 13 question-answer turns and is grounded in information from four documents. What sets our dataset apart from other ConvQA datasets is the inclusion of topic switches within the conversation.

Evaluation: The performance of TopiOCQA is measured using F1 score and Exact Match (EM). In the context of QA, these metrics are often used to assess the performance of a model in generating answers that match the reference answers. EM is more stringent, requiring an exact match, while F1 score considers partial matches, giving credit for overlapping words between the predicted and reference answers.

2.6 RESEARCH TRENDS

ConvQA is a rapidly evolving field. This section presents new approaches that have been recently utilized in our daily lives. These ConvQA systems have the potential to be successfully utilized in practical applications:

1. **Single Source of Information:** The KB-QA-based systems allow users to access a series of information via conversation without even composing complex SQL queries. From a commercial perspective, these KB-QA-based systems can be employed either in open-domain QA (pertaining to worldly knowledge) or in closed-domain QA (such as in the medical field). A user does not have to access multiple sources of information, one agent would suffice their all information needs.

2. **Conversational Search:** ConvQA systems provide simplified conversational search setting [63] that has the strongest potential to become more popular than the traditional search engines such as Google or Bing,

which, unlike a user's expectations of getting a concise answer, provides a list of probable answers/solutions. These conversational systems can potentially be used for learning about a topic, planning an activity, seeking advice or guidance, and making a decision.

3. **Customer Support System:** The conversational agents play a significant role in facilitating smooth interaction with users. One of the conceivable applications could be customer support systems where a user does not have to go through the entire website and look for the desired information.

2.7 SUMMARY

ConvQA systems have been emerging as a main technology to close the interactional gap between machines and humans owing to the advancements in pre-trained language modeling and the introduction of conversational datasets. This progress simplifies the development and progress of application areas such as online customer support, interactions with Internet of Things (IoT) devices in smart spaces, and search engines, thus enabling ConvQA to realize its social and economic impacts. The effective incorporation of contextual information, the ability to infer the questions, and ask efficient clarification questions are the main challenges in the field of ConvQA.

Our investigation of research activities over the past few years confirms the thriving expansion of this exciting field. In this chapter, we have comprehensively discussed the field of ConvQA, which is further subdivided into (i) sequential KB-QA and (ii) CMRC. The general architecture of each of the categories is decomposed into modules and prominent techniques employed in each module have been discussed with a primary focus on CMRC. Subsequently, the chapter introduces and discusses the representative ConvQA datasets based on their characteristics. Finally, the potential applications of ConvQA in different directions have been outlined and discussed briefly.

It is evident from the literature review that context modeling plays a crucial role in the performance of the model. However, the context sometimes can be implicit and incomplete, making it complicated for the model to grasp the correct interpretation of it. Accordingly, the next chapter emphasizes proposing a model to address the issue of incomplete and ambiguous follow-up questions using a few key entities from the given conversational context. Once the entities are generated, they can be utilized as a part of input to the model as an additional cue to understand an incomplete question.

References

[1] Vaibhav Adlakha et al. "TopiOCQA: Open-domain Conversational Question Answering with Topic Switching". In: *Transactions of Association for Computational Linguistics* 10 (2022).

[2] Raviteja Anantha et al. "Open-Domain Question Answering Goes Conversational via Question Rewriting". In: *Proceedings of the 2021 Conference of the North American Chapter of the Association for Computational Linguistics: Human Language Technologies, (NAACL-HLT)*. 2021, pp. 520–534.

[3] Dzmitry Bahdanau, Kyunghyun Cho, and Yoshua Bengio. "Neural Machine Translation by Jointly Learning to Align and Translate". In: *Proceedings of the 3rd International Conference on Learning Representations (ICLR)*. 2015, pp. 01–15.

[4] Ian Beaver, Cynthia Freeman, and Abdullah Mueen. "Towards Awareness of Human Relational Strategies in Virtual Agents". In: *Proceedings of the 34th Conference on Artificial Intelligence (AAAI)*. 2020, pp. 2602–2610.

[5] Nikita Bhutani et al. "Answering Complex Questions by Combining Information from Curated and Extracted Knowledge Bases". In: *Proceedings of the First Workshop on Natural Language Interfaces (NLI)*. 2020, pp. 1–10.

[6] Kurt Bollacker et al. "Freebase: A Collaboratively Created Graph Database for Structuring Human Knowledge". In: *Proceedings of the International Conference on Management of Data (SIGMOD)*. 2008, pp. 1247–1250.

[7] Abdelghani Bouziane et al. "Question Answering Systems: Survey and Trends". In: *Procedia Computer Science* 73 (2015).

[8] Paweł Budzianowski et al. "MultiWOZ - A Large-Scale Multi-Domain Wizard-of-Oz Dataset for Task-Oriented Dialogue Modelling". In: *Proceedings of the Conference on Empirical Methods in Natural Language Processing (EMNLP)*. 2018, pp. 5016–5026.

[9] Paola Cascante-Bonilla et al. "Moviescope: Large-scale Analysis of Movies using Multiple Modalities". In: *arXiv:1908.03180* (2019).

[10] Danqi Chen et al. "Reading Wikipedia to Answer Open-Domain Questions". In: *Proceedings of the 55th Annual Meeting of the Association for Computational Linguistics (ACL)*. 2017, pp. 1870–1879.

[11] Yu Chen, Lingfei Wu, and Mohammed J. Zaki. "GraphFlow: Exploiting Conversation Flow with Graph Neural Networks for Conversational Machine Comprehension". In: *Proceedings of the 29TH International Conference on Artificial Intelligence (AAAI)*. 2020, pp. 1230–1236.

[12] Eunsol Choi et al. "QuAC: Question Answering in Context". In: *Proceedings of the 2018 Conference on Empirical Methods in Natural Language Processing (EMNLP)*. 2018, pp. 2174–2184.

[13] Philipp Christmann et al. "Look Before You Hop: Conversational Question Answering over Knowledge Graphs Using Judicious Context Expansion". In: *Proceedings of the 28th ACM International Conference on Information and Knowledge Management (CIKM)*. 2019, pp. 729–738.

[14] Wanyun Cui et al. "KBQA: Learning Question Answering over QA Corpora and Knowledge Bases". In: *In Proceedings of the VLDB Endowment* 10.5 (2017).

[15] Zihang Dai et al. "Transformer-XL: Attentive Language Models beyond a Fixed-Length Context". In: *Proceedings of the 57th Conference of the Association for Computational Linguistics (ACL)*. 2019, pp. 2978–2988.

[16] Jacob Devlin et al. "BERT: Pre-training of Deep Bidirectional Transformers for Language Understanding". In: *Proceedings of the 2019 Conference of the North American Chapter of the Association for Computational Linguistics: Human Language Technologies (NAACL-HLT)*. 2019, pp. 4171–4186.

[17] Bhuwan Dhingra et al. "Towards End-to-End Reinforcement Learning of Dialogue Agents for Information Access". In: *Proceedings of the 55th Annual Meeting of the Association for Computational Linguistics (ACL)*. 2017, pp. 484–495.

[18] Ahmed Elgohary, Denis Peskov, and Jordan Boyd-Graber. "Can You Unpack That? Learning to Rewrite Questions-in-Context". In: *Proceedings of the 2019 Conference on Empirical Methods in Natural Language Processing and the 9th International Joint Conference on Natural Language Processing (EMNLP-IJCNLP)*. 2019, pp. 5918–5924.

[19] Angela Fan, Mike Lewis, and Yann N. Dauphin. "Hierarchical Neural Story Generation". In: *Proceedings of the 56th Annual Meeting of the Association for Computational Linguistics (ACL)*. 2018, pp. 889–898.

[20] Hung-Chieh Fang et al. "Open-Domain Conversational Question Answering with Historical Answers". In: *Findings of the Association for Computational Linguistics: (ACL-IJCNLP)*. 2022, pp. 319–326.

[21] Jianfeng Gao, Michel Galley, and Lihong Li. "Neural Approaches to Conversational AI". In: *Foundations and Trends in Information Retrieval* 13 (2019).

[22] Daya Guo et al. "Dialog-to-Action: conversational Question Answering Over a Large-Scale Knowledge Base". In: *Proceedings of the 32nd International Conference on Neural Information Processing Systems (NeurIPS)*. 2018, pp. 2946–2955.

[23] Somil Gupta, Bhanu Pratap Singh Rawat, and Hong Yu. "Conversational Machine Comprehension: a Literature Review". In: *Proceedings of the 28th International Conference on Computational Linguistics (COLING)*. 2020, pp. 2739–2753.

[24] Karl Moritz Hermann et al. "Teaching Machines to Read and Comprehend". In: *Proceedings of the 28th International Conference on Neural Information Processing Systems (NeurIPS)*. 2015, pp. 1693–1701.

[25] Ryuichiro Higashinaka and Hideki Isozaki. "Corpus-based Question Answering for why-Questions". In: *Proceedings of the 3rd International Joint Conference on Natural Language Processing (IJCNLP)*. 2008, pp. 01–08.

[26] Sepp Hochreiter and Jürgen Schmidhuber. "Long Short-term Memory". In: *Neural Computation* 9.8 (1997).

[27] Hsin-Yuan Huang, Eunsol Choi, and Wen-tau Yih. "FlowQA: Grasping Flow in History for Conversational Machine Comprehension". In: *Proceedings of the 7th The International Conference on Learning Representations*. 2019, pp. 86–90.

[28] Mohit Iyyer, Wen-tau Yih, and Ming-Wei Chang. "Search-based Neural Structured Learning for Sequential Question Answering". In: *Proceedings of the 55th Annual Meeting of the Association for Computational Linguistics (ACL)*. 2017, pp. 1821–1831.

[29] Mohit Iyyer et al. "A Neural Network for Factoid Question Answering over Paragraphs". In: *Proceedings of the Conference on Empirical Methods in Natural Language Processing (EMNLP)*. 2014, pp. 633–644.

[30] Soyeong Jeong et al. "Phrase Retrieval for Open Domain Conversational Question Answering with Conversational Dependency Modeling via Contrastive Learning". In: *Findings of the Association for Computational Linguistics (ACL)*. 2023, pp. 6019–6031.

[31] Kelvin Jiang, Dekun Wu, and Hui Jiang. "FreebaseQA: A New Factoid QA Data Set Matching Trivia-Style Question-Answer Pairs with Freebase". In: *Proceedings of the Conference of the North American Chapter of the Association for Computational Linguistics: Human Language Technologies (NAACL-HLT)*. 2019, pp. 318–323.

[32] Mandar Joshi et al. "SpanBERT: Improving Pretraining by Representing and Predicting Spans". In: *Transactions of the Association for Computational Linguistics (ACL)* 8 (2020).

[33] Mandar Joshi et al. "TriviaQA: A Large Scale Distantly Supervised Challenge Dataset for Reading Comprehension". In: *Proceedings of the 55th Annual Meeting of the Association for Computational Linguistics (ACL)*. 2017, pp. 1601–1611.

[34] Vladimir Karpukhin et al. "Dense Passage Retrieval for Open-Domain Question Answering". In: *Proceedings of the 2020 Conference on Empirical Methods in Natural Language Processing (EMNLP)*. 2020, pp. 6769–6781.

[35] Omar Khattab and Matei Zaharia. "ColBERT: Efficient and Effective Passage Search via Contextualized Late Interaction over BERT". In: *Proceedings of the 43rd International ACM conference on research and development in Information Retrieval (SIGIR)*. Ed. by Jimmy X. Huang et al. 2020, pp. 39–48.

[36] Tomás Kociský et al. "The NarrativeQA Reading Comprehension Challenge". In: *Transactions of the Association for Computational Linguistics* (2018).

[37] Tom Kwiatkowski et al. "Natural Questions: A Benchmark for Question Answering Research". In: *Transaction of Association for Computational Linguistics* 7 (2019).

[38] Guokun Lai et al. "RACE: large-scale ReAding Comprehension Dataset From Examinations". In: *Proceedings of the Conference on Empirical Methods in Natural Language Processing (EMNLP)*. 2017, pp. 785–794.

[39] Zhenzhong Lan et al. "ALBERT: A Lite BERT for Self-supervised Learning of Language Representations". In: *Proceedings of the 8th International Conference on Learning Representations (ICLR)*. 2020.

[40] Jens Lehmann et al. "DBpedia–A Large-scale, Multilingual Knowledge Base Extracted from Wikipedia". In: *Semantic Web* 6.2 (2015).

[41] Shanshan Liu et al. "Neural Machine Reading Comprehension: Methods and Trends". In: *Applied Sciences* 9.18 (2019).

[42] Yinhan Liu et al. "RoBERTa: A Robustly Optimized BERT Pretraining Approach". In: *CoRR* abs/1907.11692 (2019).

[43] Xiaolu Lu et al. "Answering Complex Questions by Joining Multi-Document Evidence with Quasi Knowledge Graphs". In: *Proceedings of the 42nd International Conference on Research and Development in Information Retrieval (SIGIR)*. 2019, pp. 105–114.

[44] Jorge Martinez-Gil. "Automated Knowledge Base Management: A Survey". In: *Computer Science Review* 18 (2015).

[45] Bryan McCann et al. "Learned in Translation: Contextualized Word Vectors". In: *Proceedings of the 31st International Conference on Neural Information Processing Systems (NeurIPS)*. 2017, pp. 6294–6305.

[46] Tomas Mikolov et al. "Efficient Estimation of Word Representations in Vector Space". In: *Proceedings of the 1st International Conference on Learning Representations (ICLR)*. 2013, pp. 01–12.

[47] Alexander H. Miller et al. "ParlAI: a Dialog Research Software Platform". In: *Proceedings of the Conference on Empirical Methods in Natural Language Processing (EMNLP)*. 2017, pp. 79–84.

[48] Amit Mishra and Sanjay Kumar Jain. "A Survey on Question Answering Systems With Classification". In: *Journal of King Saud University-Computer and Information Sciences* 28.3 (2016).

[49] Tom Mitchell et al. "Never-ending Learning". In: *Communications of the ACM* 61.5 (2018).

[50] Christof Monz. "Machine Learning for Query Formulation in Question Answering". In: *Natural Language Engineering* 17.4 (2011).

[51] Thomas Müller et al. "Answering Conversational Questions on Structured Data without Logical Forms". In: *Proceedings of the Conference on Empirical Methods in Natural Language Processing and the 9th International Joint Conference on Natural Language Processing (EMNLP-IJCNLP)*. 2019, pp. 5901–5909.

[52] Ramesh Nallapati et al. "Abstractive Text Summarization using Sequence-to-sequence RNNs and Beyond". In: *Proceedings of the 20th Conference on Computational Natural Language Learning (CoNLL)*. 2016, pp. 280–290.

[53] Tri Nguyen et al. "MS MARCO: A Human Generated MAchine Reading COmprehension Dataset". In: *Proceedings of the 30th Annual Conference on Neural Information Processing Systems (NeurIPS)*. 2016, pp. 01–11.

[54] Yasuhito Ohsugi et al. "A Simple but Effective Method to Incorporate Multi-turn Context with BERT for Conversational Machine Comprehension". In: *Proceedings of the 57th Annual Meeting of the Association for Computational Linguistics (ACL)*. 2019, pp. 11–17.

[55] Simon Ostermann et al. "MCScript: a Novel Dataset for Assessing Machine Comprehension Using Script Knowledge". In: *Proceedings of the 11th International Conference on Language Resources and Evaluation (LREC)*. 2018, pp. 01–08.

[56] Jeffrey Pennington, Richard Socher, and Christopher Manning. "GloVe: Global Vectors for Word Representation". In: *Proceedings of the Conference on Empirical Methods in Natural Language Processing (EMNLP)*. 2014, pp. 1532–1543.

[57] Matthew Peters et al. "Deep Contextualized Word Representations". In: *Proceedings of the Conference of the North American Chapter of the Association for Computational Linguistics: Human Language Technologies (NAACL-HLT)*. 2018, pp. 2227–2237.

[58] David Pinto et al. "Quasm: A System for Question Answering using Semi-structured Data". In: *Proceedings of the 2nd ACM/IEEE-CS Joint Conference on Digital Libraries*. 2002, pp. 46–55.

[59] Peng Qi et al. "Answering Complex Open-domain Questions Through Iterative Query Generation". In: *Proceedings of the Conference on Empirical Methods in Natural Language Processing and the 9th International Joint Conference on Natural Language Processing (EMNLP-IJCNLP)*. 2019, pp. 2590–2602.

[60]   Minghui Qiu et al. "Reinforced History Backtracking for Conversational Question Answering". In: *Proceedings of the 35th Conference on Artificial Intelligence (AAAI)*. 2021.

[61]   Xipeng Qiu et al. "Pre-trained Models for Natural Language Processing: A Survey". In: *CoRR* abs/2003.08271 (2020). arXiv: 2003.08271.

[62]   Chen Qu et al. "Attentive History Selection for Conversational Question Answering". In: *Proceedings of the 28th ACM International Conference on Information and Knowledge Management (CIKM)*. 2019, pp. 1391–1400.

[63]   Chen Qu et al. "BERT with History Answer Embedding for Conversational Question Answering". In: *Proceedings of the 42nd International ACM Conference on Research and Development in Information Retrieval (SIGIR)*. 2019, pp. 1133–1136.

[64]   Chen Qu et al. "Open-retrieval Conversational Question Answering". In: *Proceedings of the 43rd International Conference on Research and Development in Information Retrieval (SIGIR)*. 2020, pp. 539–548.

[65]   Chen Qu et al. "Weakly-Supervised Open-Retrieval Conversational Question Answering". In: *Proceedings of the 43rd European Conference on Information Retrieval Research*. 2021, pp. 529–543.

[66]   Alec Radford et al. "Improving Language Understanding by Generative Pre-training". In: *OpenAI Blog* 2.5 (2018).

[67]   Alec Radford et al. "Language Models Are Unsupervised Multitask Learners". In: *OpenAI Blog* 1.8 (2019), p. 9.

[68]   Pranav Rajpurkar, Robin Jia, and Percy Liang. "Know What You Don't Know: Unanswerable Questions for SQuAD". In: *Proceedings of the 56th Annual Meeting*

of the Association for Computational Linguistics (ACL). 2018, pp. 784–789.

[69] Pranav Rajpurkar et al. "SQuAD: 100, 000+ Questions for Machine Comprehension of Text". In: *Proceedings of the Conference on Empirical Methods in Natural Language Processing (EMNLP).* 2016, pp. 2383–2392.

[70] Siva Reddy, Danqi Chen, and Christopher D. Manning. "CoQA: A Conversational Question Answering Challenge". In: *Transaction of Association for the Computational Linguistics* 7 (2019), pp. 1–8.

[71] Liliang Ren et al. "Towards Universal Dialogue State Tracking". In: *Proceedings of the Conference on Empirical Methods in Natural Language Processing (EMNLP).* 2018, pp. 2780–2786.

[72] Matthew Richardson, Christopher J. C. Burges, and Erin Renshaw. "MCTest: A Challenge Dataset for the Open-Domain Machine Comprehension of Text". In: *Proceedings of the Conference on Empirical Methods in Natural Language Processing (EMNLP).* 2013, pp. 193–203.

[73] Anna Rogers, Olga Kovaleva, and Anna Rumshisky. "A Primer in BERTology: What We Know About How BERT Works". In: *Transactions of Associations for Computational Linguistics* 8 (2020).

[74] David E Rumelhart, Geoffrey E Hinton, and Ronald J Williams. "Learning Representations by Back-propagating Errors". In: *Nature* 323.6088 (1986).

[75] Marzieh Saeidi et al. "Interpretation of Natural Language Rules in Conversational Machine Reading". In: *Proceedings of the Conference on Empirical Methods in Natural Language Processing (EMNLP).* 2018, pp. 2087–2097.

[76] Amrita Saha et al. "Complex Sequential Question Answering: towards Learning to Converse Over Linked Question Answer Pairs with a Knowledge Graph". In: *Proceedings of the 32nd Conference on Artificial Intelligence (AAAI)*. 2018, pp. 705–713.

[77] Abigail See, Peter J. Liu, and Christopher D. Manning. "Get To The Point: Summarization with Pointer-Generator Networks". In: *Proceedings of the 55th Annual Meeting of the Association for Computational Linguistics (ACL)*. 2017, pp. 1073–1083.

[78] Min Joon Seo et al. "Bidirectional Attention Flow for Machine Comprehension". In: *5th International Conference on Learning Representations (ICLR)*. 2017.

[79] Dan Shen and Dietrich Klakow. "Exploring Correlation of Dependency Relation Paths for Answer Extraction". In: *Proceedings of the 44th Annual Meeting of the Association for Computational Linguistics (ACL)*. 2006, pp. 889–896.

[80] Alane Suhr, Srinivasan Iyer, and Yoav Artzi. "Learning to Map Context-Dependent Sentences to Executable Formal Queries". In: *Proceedings of the Conference of the North American Chapter of the Association for Computational Linguistics: Human Language Technologies (NAACL-HLT)*. 2018, pp. 2238–2249.

[81] Rui Sun et al. "Multi-modal Knowledge Graphs for Recommender Systems". In: *Proceedings of the 29th ACM International Conference on Information & Knowledge Management (CIKM)*. 2020, pp. 1405–1414.

[82] Ilya Sutskever, Oriol Vinyals, and Quoc V Le. "Sequence to Sequence Learning with Neural Networks". In: *Proceeding of the Advances in Neural Information Processing Systems (NeurIPS)*. Vol. 27. 2014, pp. 3104–3112.

[83] Zhiliang Tian et al. "How to Make Context More Useful? An Empirical Study on Context-Aware Neural Conversational Models". In: *Proceedings of the 55th Annual Meeting of the Association for Computational Linguistics (ACL)*. 2017, pp. 231–236.

[84] Adam Trischler et al. "NewsQA: a Machine Comprehension Dataset". In: *Proceedings of the 55th Annual Meeting of the Association for Computational Linguistics (ACL)*. 2017, pp. 191–200.

[85] Priyansh Trivedi et al. "LC-QuAD: A Corpus for Complex Question Answering over Knowledge Graphs". In: *Proceedings of the 16th International Semantic Web Conference (ISWC)*. 2017, pp. 210–218.

[86] Ashish Vaswani et al. "Attention is All you Need". In: *Proceedings of the 31st International Conference on Neural Information Processing Systems (NeurIPS)*. Vol. 30. 2017, pp. 5998–6008.

[87] Hao Wang et al. "A Neural Question Answering Model Based on Semi-Structured Tables". In: *Proceedings of the 27th International Conference on Computational Linguistics*. 2018, pp. 1941–1951.

[88] Johannes Welbl, Nelson F. Liu, and Matt Gardner. "Crowdsourcing Multiple Choice Science Questions". In: *Proceedings of the Conference on Empirical Methods in Natural Language Processing (EMNLP)*. 2017, pp. 94–106.

[89] Tsung-Hsien Wen et al. "A Network-based End-to-End Trainable Task-oriented Dialogue System". In: *Proceedings of the 15th Conference of the European Chapter of the Association for Computational Linguistics (EACL)*. 2017, pp. 438–449.

[90] Ji Wu, Miao Li, and Chin-Hui Lee. "A Probabilistic Framework for Representing Dialog Systems and Entropy-based Dialog Management Through Dynamic Stochastic State Evolution". In: *IEEE/ACM*

Transactions on Audio, Speech, and Language Processing 23.11 (2015).

[91] Wenhan Xiong et al. "Answering Complex Open-Domain Questions with Multi-Hop Dense Retrieval". In: *Proceedings of the 9th International Conference on Learning Representations (ICLR)*. 2021, pp. 01–19.

[92] Yi Yang, Wen-tau Yih, and Christopher Meek. "WikiQA: A Challenge Dataset for Open-Domain Question Answering". In: *Proceedings of the Conference on Empirical Methods in Natural Language Processing (EMNLP)*. 2015, pp. 2013–2018.

[93] Zhilin Yang et al. "XLNet: Generalized Autoregressive Pretraining for Language Understanding". In: *Advances in Neural Information Processing Systems 32: Annual Conference on Neural Information Processing Systems 2019 (NeurIPS)*. 2019, pp. 5754–5764.

[94] Mark Yatskar. "A Qualitative Comparison of CoQA, SQuAD 2.0 and QuAC". In: *Proceedings of the Conference of the North American Chapter of the Association for Computational Linguistics: Human Language Technologies (NAACL-HLT)*. 2019, pp. 2318–2323.

[95] Yi-Ting Yeh and Yun-Nung Chen. "FlowDelta: Modeling Flow Information Gain in Reasoning for Conversational Machine Comprehension". In: *Proceedings of the 2nd Workshop on Machine Reading for Question Answering*. 2019, pp. 86–90.

[96] Shi Yu et al. "Few-Shot Conversational Dense Retrieval". In: *The 44th International ACM Conference on Research and Development in Information Retrieval (SIGIR)*. Ed. by Fernando Diaz et al. 2021, pp. 829–838.

[97] Munazza Zaib, Quan Z. Sheng, and Wei Emma Zhang. "A Short Survey of Pre-trained Language Models for Conversational AI-A New Age in NLP". In: *Proceedings of the Australasian Computer Science Week (ACSW)*. 2020, 11:1–11:4.

[98] Yongfeng Zhang et al. "Towards Conversational Search and Recommendation: System Ask, User Respond". In: *Proceedings of the 27th ACM International Conference on Information and Knowledge Management (CIKM)*. 2018, pp. 177–186.

[99] Chenguang Zhu, Michael Zeng, and Xuedong Huang. "SDNet: contextualized Attention-based Deep Network for Conversational Question Answering". In: *arXiv:1812.03593* (2018).

[100] Xiaohan Zou. "A Survey on Application of Knowledge Graph". In: *Proceedings of the 4th International Conference on Control Engineering and Artificial Intelligence (CCEAI)*. Vol. 1487. 2020, p. 012016.

CHAPTER 3

Resolving Conversational Dependencies in Conversational Question Answering

Having an intelligent dialog agent that can engage in ConvQA is no longer limited to Sci-Fi movies only and has turned into a reality. These intelligent agents are required to understand and correctly interpret the sequential turns provided as the *context* of the given question. However, these sequential questions are sometimes left implicit and thus require the resolution of some natural language phenomena such as *anaphora* and *ellipsis*. The task of question rewriting has the potential to address the challenges of resolving dependencies among the contextual turns by transforming them into *intent-explicit questions*. Nonetheless, the solution of rewriting the implicit questions comes with some potential challenges such as resulting in verbose questions and taking *conversational* aspect out of the scenario by generating

DOI: 10.1201/9781003592068-3

the self-contained questions. In this chapter[1], a novel framework for capturing and generating intermediate representations as conversational cues to enhance the capability of the QA model to better interpret incomplete questions is proposed. This work also deliberate how the strengths of this task could be leveraged in a bid to design more engaging and more eloquent conversational agents. The model has been tested on the QuAC and CANARD datasets and illustrated by experimental results that our proposed framework achieves a better F1 score than the standard question rewriting model.

3.1 OVERVIEW

ConvQA is a relatively new paradigm and considerable task that possesses the potential to revolutionize the way humans interact with machines [29]. It, in fact, requires a system to answer a set of interrelated questions posed by any user [3, 21, 7]. In human conversations, these sequential questions could be *implicit* and are very easy for them to understand [4]. However, ConvQA-based machines are expected to learn and resolve such implicit dependencies from the given context. For instance, let us consider a ConvQA session pertinent to a TV show in Table 3.1. To interpret and answer Q2, the system is expected to have information about Q1 and A1. Similarly, it would be difficult for the system to find the answer to Q3 since there could be many first seasons of different series. To retrieve the correct answer, the system needs to incorporate the show name in the question.

Furthermore, the task of question rewriting (QR) has been extensively researched upon by researchers in the information extraction community. Nevertheless, it is fairly new in the field of ConvQA and is recently introduced as an independent task in some ConvQA models [23, 27, 10].

---

[1]This work has been published in [30].

TABLE 3.1   An Example of Information-Seeking Dialog

Topic: F.R.I.E.N.D.S	
ID	**Conversation**
Q1	Who played Monica Geller in FRIENDS?
A1	Courteney Cox.
Q2	What was she obsessed about?
A2	Cleaning.
Q3	Who was the noisy neighbor?
A3	Larry Hankin
Q4	Release date of the first season?
A4	September 22, 1994.

Red denotes the context entity, whereas blue represents the question entities.

Simply put, QR refers to the task of reformulating the given question by adding missing information or resolving co-references. This process generates a stand-alone question by extracting it out of the conversational context [20]. However, this results in losing valuable cues from the conversational flow. Also, the resulting rephrased questions might be long and verbose which, in turn, results in difficulty in retrieving evidence from the given context. Furthermore, the datasets available for QR in ConvQA are quite small, thereby hindering the training process of the model.

To address these particular shortcomings, an ensemble model entitled, CONVSR (**CONV**QA using **S**tructured **R**epresentations), has been proposed which instead of rewriting an incomplete or ambiguous question generates the intermediate structured representations (SR) based on the given context and the question. These representations, comprising the context and the question entities, can ultimately be used to fill up the missing gaps and answer the question at hand. The key intuition behind such a model is that an incomplete question only needs to refer to the last few questions in order to fill in the missing gaps because the conversational flow keeps on changing [8, 17, 26]. Hence, to accommodate the changing conversational flow, we propose to select k history turns using a dynamic history selection process.

Some questions would require both the context and the question entities in a bid to disambiguate the current question, whereas, for some questions, only the context entities would be enough. For instance, to answer Q2 in Table 3.1, the model needs to refer back to the intermediate representations captured for Q1. In this case, the model needs to have both the context entity (FRIENDS) and the question entity (Monica Geller) to decipher *"she"* in Q2. However, to answer Q4, the model only needs the context entity, i.e., FRIENDS.

Hence, the proposed model consists of the following main stages: *(i) Question understanding* that encompasses assessing a question based on the given context; *(ii) Dynamic history selection* that conducts "hard selection" for the relevant history turns. This method attends to the previous history turns based on a semantic similarity score. If a conversational turn equals or surpasses a threshold value, then it is considered important for predicting the answer; *(iii) Entity generation* that works toward identifying the context and question entities (if any) from the selected history turns; and *(iv) Answer prediction* that retrieves the most relevant answer span from the given context based on the selected history turns and their respective SRs.

In a nutshell, the technical contributions of this research work are summarized as the following:

1. It highlights the constraints of preceding methods and introduces a framework aimed at overcoming these limitations. The proposed framework presents an alternative of QR task to complete the ambiguous questions by generating intermediate structured representations.

2. A dynamic history selection policy based on "hard history selection" has been envisaged to select only the relevant subset of conversational turns.

3. The effect of SRs has been studied on traditional ConvQA baselines by skipping the dynamic history selection process and appending the history turns in different settings.

4. It is demonstrated by the experimental results that a decline in accuracy is experienced by ConvQA models when QR tasks are incorporated within the model, thus proving the effectiveness of our approach.

To the best of our knowledge, the proposed research is one of the few research works that implement the task of question resolution within the ConvQA setting.

The rest of this chapter is organized as follows. Section 3.2 overviews the techniques of (ConvQA) and question completion. Section 3.3 illustrates the technical details pertinent to our proposed CONVSR model. Section 3.4 describes the experimental setup and Section 3.5 reports the experimental results. Finally, Section 3.6 offers some concluding remarks.

3.2 STATE OF THE ART

3.2.1 Conversational Question Answering

The task of ConvQA presents several challenges to the researchers, hence resulting in considerable interesting yet innovative research works over the past few years. One of the key challenges in the task of ConvQA is to incorporate the conversational history effectively so that the model can best interpret the current question accurately. Some popular strategies include prepending the conversational turns [3, 21, 15] and dynamic history selection either utilizing attention mechanism [17] or reward-based reinforcement learning [16]. Several other works also demonstrate the effectiveness of FLOW-based mechanisms [26, 8, 1] to capture the intermediate latent representations to help the answering process. We employ a dynamic history selection process to obtain question-relevant conversation history turns. Integrating non-relevant conversational turns tend to bring noise into the input provided to the model, which in turn, results in the model's performance degradation [28, 17, 16]. The process is based on hard history selection and will be discussed in Section 3.3.

3.2.2 Question Completion

A popular research direction that aims to address the challenges pertinent to an incomplete or ambiguous question is QR. The task of QR is recently adopted in the field of ConvQA to rephrase and generate a self-contained question that can be answered from the given context [20, 24, 10, 6, 12, 2, 9]. However, the task of QR takes the conversational questions out of context by transforming them into self-contained questions, which in turn, negates the whole idea of ConvQA setting [4]. Question resolution is another approach that adds relevant and significant terms from the previous conversation turns to fill in the missing information gaps [25]. These techniques are widely used to resolve co-dependencies and anaphora among the conversational history turns.

This research work focuses on the second type of question completion technique and shows in the experimental results in Section 3.5 that question reformulation with added valuable cues performs better than rewriting questions from scratch.

3.3 METHODOLOGY

3.3.1 Task Formulation

The research work assumes the traditional setting of ConvQA where a user starts the conversation with a particular question or information need and the system searches the given context to provide an answer after each of the user's questions [28]. The follow-up questions may be incomplete or ambiguous requiring more context to be interpreted by the model. The task of CONVSR is to capture the context

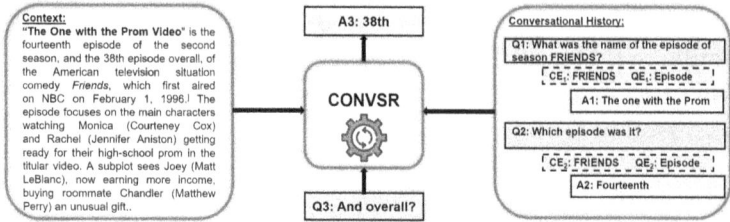

FIGURE 3.1 An illustration of the proposed model Conversational Question Answering with Structured Representations (CONVSR). CE and QE in CONVSR denote the context entity and question entity.

entities and question entities from the previous relevant conversation turns and utilize them as additional cues to answer incomplete questions. The term *context entity (CE)* corresponds to an entity mentioned in the previous conversational context and the term *question entity (QE)* corresponds to the entities given in the previous questions. Essentially, an SR consisting of CE and QE for any given question can be represented as shown in Figure. 3.1.

More formally, given a passage p, previous history turns h and a potentially ambiguous or incomplete question q which may need the understanding of the previous conversation turns, the task of CONVSR is to first select the relevant history turns h' and then capture the structured representations SR in the form CE and QE. These SRs are then infused into the ConvQA model to be utilized to generate the correct answer a. An illustration of the proposed model CONVSR is depicted in Figure. 3.1.

3.3.2 Pipeline Approach

Over the past few years, a number of research works [10, 23, 20, 22] have envisaged various models to tackle the complexity of ConvQA task by decomposing it into QR and QA subtasks. Question rewriting, being the initial sub-task, generates self-contained questions by rewriting the given incomplete question from scratch. Different approaches are in use to generate these rewrites such as language models [20, 22, 13] and neural networks [23]. The QR models are trained on a recently introduced CANARD [6] dataset, which is based on QuAC's [3] original questions and their respective rewrites. The dataset has around 40K question pairs generated by human annotators.

Following [13], the proposed model adopts GPT-2 [19] to train the QR model. In the training process, the model is provided with the conversational turns and the current question as the inputs and the model generates a context-independent rewrite that is to be answered without considering the conversational history. Once the rewrites are generated, the next sub-task is of the QA module to find a relevant answer from the given context. Since it is assumed that all the co-references and anaphoras have been resolved in the QR task, most research works employ a traditional QA model instead of the ConvQA framework to answer the current question. However, the conversational history is utilized along with SRs in the proposed model, therefore, for a fair comparison, we also utilize conversational history along with the rewritten question as input to the QA model. The process of predicting an answer can be put together as:

$$P = (a_i, |q_i, P, H) \approx P^{qr}(q_i'|q_i, h) \cdot P^{qa}(a_i|q', p, h) \qquad (3.1)$$

where $P^{qr}(\cdot)$ and $P^{qa}(\cdot)$ are the likelihood functions of the two sub-task models, respectively. q' represents the rewritten question by the QR model and it serves as an input to the QA model along with the given context and history turns. The pipeline model is shown in Fig. 3.2a. The dotted line represents that conversational history forms an input to the ConvQA model along with the rewritten question.

The primary limitation of using this approach is that the QA model never gets to be trained on the user's actual questions, and tends to lose the understanding of the conversational context. Also, the input of a QA model is highly

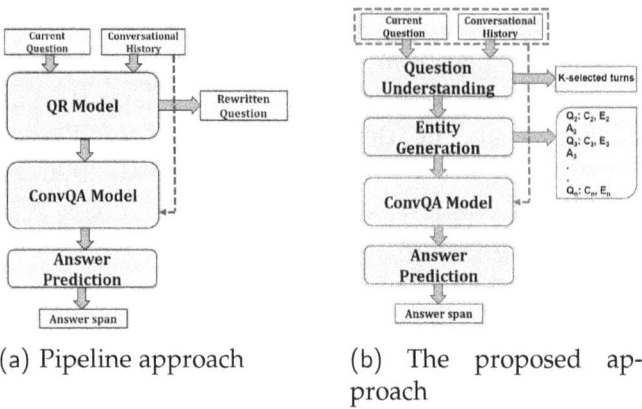

(a) Pipeline approach

(b) The proposed approach

FIGURE 3.2 In the pipeline approach, a context-independent question is generated by the QR model that serves as an input to the ConvQA model to predict an answer span. In our approach, the first relevant history turns are selected and SRs are generated for them. The SRs, current question, and history turns to form an input for the QA model to find the accurate answer.

dependent on the output of the QR model, which increases the chances of QA model being suffered by error propagation from QR model.

3.3.3 The CONVSR Model

Follow-up questions in a conversation are usually incomplete and require explicit information to identify the question's intent. Thus, the key challenge pertinent to ConvQA involves understanding the conversational flow to derive the structured representations to aid the answering process of the user's information need. Instead of following the conventional approach of QR, this work rather aims to capture and extract intermediate SRs to keep the task conversational. These SRs serve as an aid to an incomplete question by filling in the gap by adding more context using context entity and/or by resolving co-references using question entity.

Algorithm 1 The Proposed Model-CONVSR

1: **Input:** Current Question (q), Passage (p), History Turns (h),
2: **Output:** a: Correct Answer
   Selected Turns
3: $h' = \{\}$
4: $j = 0, N = Number\ of\ Turns/Questions$
5: **for** $i \in N$ **do**
6:   Compute   Features   Similarity: $s_{i,j}$ $=$
     $similarity(feature_i, feature_j)$
7:   $Softcosine(q, h) = \dfrac{\sum_{i,j}^{N} s_{i,j}\ q_i\ h_j}{\sqrt{\sum_{i,j}^{N} s_{i,j}q_iq_j}\sqrt{\sum_{i,j}^{i-1} s_{i,j}h_ih_j}}$
8:   **if** $Softcosine(q_i, h_i) >= 0.75$ **then**
9:     $h' = Softcosine(q_i, h_i)$
10:   **end if**
11: **end for**
    Entity Generation
12: $CE, QE = BART(q_i[SEP]h_j^{N-1})$
    ConvQA Model
13: **if** $An\ Ambiguous\ Followup\ Question$ **then**
14:   Use CE, QE from Previous Turns
15: **else**
16:   Continue
17: **end if**
18: **return** Correct Answer a

However, generating SR for all the previous questions would bring in the noise data (irrelevant information), which tends to decrease the model's performance as proved in [28, 18]. Also, the follow-up questions usually take their context and question entities from the previous immediate turns. The dialog behavior of *topic shift* and *topic return* requires the explicit mention of the new entity and the context.

We propose Algorithm 1 based on intermediate structured representations that summarize the workflow of

CONVSR model. The proposed model utilize a pre-trained seq2seq language model, BART [11] to perform history selection and generate SR entities. It consists of both an encoder and a decoder. The model is best utilized when the information is duplicated from the input but manipulated to produce the result autoregressively [11], which is exactly the case here. The input to the model is the current question with previous conversational turns concatenated with a delimiter and the output consists of the structured representations. Once the input has been encoded, we calculate the soft cosine similarity between the current question and the given history turns. Unlike regular cosine similarity (which would result in zero for vectors with no overlapping terms), soft cosine similarity considers word similarity as well. The resultant value for soft cosine similarity ranges from 0 to 1 where 0 is no match and 1 represents an exact match with the history turns. Soft cosine similarity can be calculated as:

$$Softcosine(q, h) = \frac{\sum_{i,j}^{N} s_{i,j} \, q_i \, h_j}{\sqrt{\sum_{i,j}^{N} s_{i,j} q_i q_j} \sqrt{\sum_{i,j}^{i-1} s_{i,j} h_i h_j}} \quad (3.2)$$

where q_i is the current question, h_j^N represents history turns (j is equivalent to 0 and N is equivalent to $i-1$), and $s_{i,j} = similarity(feature_i, feature_j)$.

We perform different experiments and conclude that the turns surpassing the threshold value of 0.75 contribute more to predicting the current answer span. Thus, all the turns that do not meet the threshold value would be filtered out. The resultant vectors are now passed on to the decoder to generate context and question entities for the respective turn. These entities are self-contained representations that capture the user's conversation flow from the previous history turns.

Once the SRs are generated for the previous history turns, the next step is to integrate them with the current question and the given context to provide some additional cues to answer the question. The architecture of CONVSR is shown in Figure. 3.2b. The dotted line represents that both the current question and conversational history form part of an input along with SRs to the ConvQA model.

3.4 EXPERIMENTAL SETUP

In this section, we describe the experimental setup for our proposed model and the pipeline approach and compare our framework to the other state-of-the-art models.

3.4.1 Dataset Description

3.4.1.1 *QuAC*

Question Answering in Context (QuAC) [3] consists of 100k question-answer pairs in a teacher-student information-seeking setting. The student seeks information on a topic provided with some background information, and the teacher attempts to satisfy the student's information need by engaging into a conversation. Since the test set is not made publicly available, we randomly distribute 5% of conversational dialogues in the training set following the strategy described in [10]. The model, then, utilize the distributed chunk as our validation set and report the test results.

3.4.1.2 CANARD

CANARD [6], a dataset based on QuAC, consists of 40k question-answer pairs. The main idea behind CANARD is to convert the context-dependent questions of QuAC into context-independent or self-contained questions. These rewritten questions have similar answers to that of the original questions. The proposed model utilizes the training and development sets for training and validating the QR model, and the test set for evaluating the ConvQA models.

3.4.2 Training and Finetuning

Since there is no training data available to generate the intermediate representations, we follow the technique of distantly supervised labeling to train the entity generation module of the model. The idea behind the technique is based on an intuition that if a piece of information (either entity or context) is essential for interpreting the follow-up question and has been omitted implicitly by the user, then it should be added to the completed version of the question. Based on this idea, the data for training is generated. We start with the complete questions and gather all the context and question entity mentions from it. For the incomplete or ambiguous follow-up questions, the model keeps on adding these entities to fill in the missing information. The entities are considered to be relevant for the incomplete question if an answer span is retrieved by adding them [4]. For training and evaluating the QR model, the model makes use of two publicly available datasets. CANARD [6] is utilized by QR module following the strategies discussed in [23, 13]. The ConvQA models are trained on the QuAC [3] dataset with Adam optimizer with a learning rate of $3e$-5.

3.4.3 ConvQA Models

Since both pipeline and CONVSR are model-agnostic, any ConvQA model can be utilized in the framework. The chosen models are widely utilized for comparison and have been proven to be performing well in ConvQA setting. We test the same models in both approaches to have a fair evaluation:

- BERT [5]: BERT is a pre-trained contextualized word representation model that is known to have empirically powerful results on different natural language tasks. BERT also works well on ConvQA datasets, although it was not designed for the task of ConvQA. It receives the context passage, current question, and conversational history as input.

- BERT-HAE [18]: BERT-HAE is based on BERT and introduces the idea of history answer embeddings to model the conversational history. These contextualized history answer embeddings encode the answer tokens from the previous turns into the model.

- RoBERTa [14]: BERT is improved using advanced pre-training strategies to get the robustly optimized weights on huge corpora and the model is named as RoBERTa. It takes the same input as BERT unless stated otherwise.

Apart from evaluating the above models with dynamic history selection, the experiments are also conducted with the traditional ConvQA setting where the history turns with no selection criteria whatsoever are appended to the current question.

Prepending previous conversational turns to the current question and the given context is still considered a simple yet very efficacious baseline in almost all ConvQA tasks. Hence, we experiment with the same here as well. Within prepending the conversational turns, we further investigate the effect of prepending only the initial turn (*prepend init*), prepending only the last turn (*prepend prev*), prepending initial and last history turns (*prepend init + prev*), and prepending all the history turns (*prepend all*). For all these other experiments, we leverage RoBERTa [14] to be the base model and adapt it according to the task. The reason for choosing RoBERTa as a base model is that it is a top-performing model on the leaderboard of different conversational datasets and has shown its effectiveness in the ConvQA domain.

3.4.4 Evaluation Metrics

For evaluation purposes, the model follows the metrics used in [3] to assess the performance of the models on the QuAC and CANARD datasets. The metrics include not only the F1 score but also the human equivalence score for questions (HEQ-Q) and dialogues (HEQ-D). HEQ-Q is the measure of the model's performance in retrieving the more accurate (or at least similar) answers for a given question. HEQ-D

TABLE 3.2   Performance Evaluation of the Pipeline Approach and CON-
VSR Using the QuAC and CANARD Datasets.

Models	Approach	F1	HEQ-Q	HEQ-D
BERT	Pipeline	61.4	57.4	5.3
	Ours	**62.7** (+1.3)	**59.2** (+1.8)	**6.2** (+0.9)
BERT-HAE	Pipeline	61.5	57.1	6.0
	Ours	**63.6** (+2.1)	**59.3** (+2.2)	**6.1** (+0.1)
RoBERTa	Pipeline	66.1	61.2	7.2
	Ours	**67.9** (+1.8)	**65.1** (+3.9)	**9.2** (+2.0)

The best scores are highlighted in bold.

represents the same performance measure but instead of a question, it evaluates the overall dialog.

3.5 RESULTS AND ANALYSIS

The experiments are conducted on CONVSR and a traditional pipeline model on different competing baselines using the QuAC and CANARD datasets. The results are reported in this section.

3.5.1 CONVSR Is Viable for Addressing Incomplete Questions in ConvQA

The first and foremost takeaway from the experiments is that the model works well in the ConvQA setting. The experiments are particularly designed to tackle the problem of incomplete or ambiguous questions. Instead of re-writing the questions to fill in the missing gaps in the given question, CONVSR generates intermediate representations based on context and question entities. These entities aid the answering process by providing cues to interpret the questions. From Table 3.2, we can clearly see that CONVSR consistently improves the model on both datasets. The model benefits by the added information cues to get a better grasp of the question-at-hand without compromising on the conversational nature of the ConvQA task.

TABLE 3.3 The Evaluation Results Based on Traditional Prepend Baselines with SRs.

Models	Approach	F1	HEQ-Q	HEQ-D
PREPEND INIT + SR	Pipeline	59.4	57.5	4.7
	Ours	**60.2** (+0.8)	**58.7** (+1.2)	**4.9** (+0.2)
PREPEND PREV + SR	Pipeline	62.2	60.1	6.0
	Ours	**64.4** (+2.2)	**63.0** (+2.9)	**7.2** (+1.2)
PREPEND INIT + PREV + SR	Pipeline	60.1	57.9	5.8
	Ours	**61.9** (+1.8)	**59.3** (+1.4)	**6.0** (+0.2)
PREPEND ALL	Pipeline	61.0	58.1	6.2
	Ours	**62.4** (+1.4)	**60.2** (+2.1)	**6.6** (+0.4)

The framework utilizes RoBERTa based model to generate the answers. The best scores are highlighted in bold.

TABLE 3.4 The Evaluation Results are Based on Traditional Prepend Baselines Without SRs.

Models	Approach	F1	HEQ-Q	HEQ-D
PREPEND INIT w/o SR	Pipeline	55.4	54.5	4.4
	Ours	**58.9** (+3.4)	**56.7** (+2.2)	**4.8** (+0.4)
PREPEND PREV w/o SR	Pipeline	58.3	56.4	6.2
	Ours	**60.1** (+1.8)	**57.2** (+0.8)	6.0 (-0.2)
PREPEND INIT + PREV w/o SR	Pipeline	57.9	55.5	5.4
	Ours	**60.2** (+2.4)	**58.4** (+2.9)	**5.9** (+0.5)
PREPEND ALL	Pipeline	58.0	58.7	6.1
	Ours	**60.0** (+2.0)	**59.4** (+0.7)	**6.4** (+0.3)

The framework utilizes RoBERTa-based model to generate the answers. The best scores are highlighted in bold.

3.5.2 CONVSR Outperforms All the Traditional Baselines

It is evident from Table 3.3 that generating SRs yields better results even in the traditional prepend baselines. Out of all the variations, *prepend prev* provides the highest F1 score. It confirms the intuition that incomplete questions usually take the context and entities of the last question asked to fill in the missing information gap. *Prepend init* results in a low F1 score mainly because of the reason that the flow of the conversation keeps on changing. The first question

TABLE 3.5   The Effect of Length on the Accuracy Score of Predicted Answer

Methods	Avg Length	Pronoun	Proper Noun	F1
Original + SR	5.5	0.5	1	67.9
Question rewriting	9	0	2.5	66.1

asked in the conversation does not necessarily provide the related context and question entities to the current question. Table 3.4 shows the accuracy scores without utilizing SRs in traditional prepend baselines. Comparing the two tables, we can clearly see that SRs provide an edge to the model in predicting correct answer spans.

3.5.3   Verbose Questions Lead to Decline in F1 Score

The results in Table 3.5 show that question re-writing results in lengthy questions, which may cause losing valuable cues from the conversation flow, hence, the decline in results. Also, QR results in more proper nouns, which shows that generating QRs requires mapping more entities within the given context. This mapping adds more complexity in generating questions from scratch.

3.6   SUMMARY

In this chapter, it is argued that generating the paraphrases of incomplete and ambiguous questions can take out questions from the conversational context, thereby impeding the underlying essence of ConvQA. Moreover, the rewritten questions are lengthy and verbose and, thus, add complexity to the answer retrieval part. In an attempt to overcome these issues, the proposed CONVSR model utilizes structured representations in the form of both context entity and question entity for predicting the answer span. The experimental results demonstrate the significance of structured representation (SR) generation within a ConvQA setting. CONVSR significantly improves ConvQA performance on both QuAC and CANARD datasets, i.e., as compared to the existing state-of-the-art. The proposed approach leverages strategies from different research fields and their strategic paradigms. The idea of generating intent-explicit SRs is taken from symbolic AI, whereas the tasks of QR and question answering have their roots embedded in the IR community.

The pipeline model stated in Section 3.3 often suffers from added noise due to the irrelevant context, resulting from a very basic history selection strategy, being introduced as a part of the input, which results in performance degradation of the model. Therefore, it is imperative to propose a dynamic history selection mechanism that considers different aspects when filtering out the irrelevant context. As a perspective, in the next chapter, the aim is to propose a more intuitive model that uses the structured representations introduced in this chapter along with attention-based re-ranking and binary term classification to carefully curate the relevant context for a ConvQA model to aid the span selection process.

References

[1] Yu Chen, Lingfei Wu, and Mohammed J. Zaki. "GraphFlow: Exploiting Conversation Flow with Graph Neural Networks for Conversational Machine Comprehension". In: *Proceedings of the 29TH International Conference on Artificial Intelligence (AAAI)*. 2020, pp. 1230–1236.

[2] Zhiyu Chen et al. "Reinforced Question Rewriting for Conversational Question Answering". In: *Proceedings of the 2022 Conference on Empirical Methods in Natural Language Processing (EMNLP)*. 2022, pp. 357–370.

[3] Eunsol Choi et al. "QuAC: Question Answering in Context". In: *Proceedings of the 2018 Conference on Empirical Methods in Natural Language Processing (EMNLP)*. 2018, pp. 2174–2184.

[4] Philipp Christmann, Rishiraj Saha Roy, and Gerhard Weikum. "Conversational Question Answering on Heterogeneous Sources". In: *Proceedings of the 45th ACM International Conference on Research and Development in Information Retrieval (SIGIR)*. 2022, pp. 144–154.

[5] Jacob Devlin et al. "BERT: Pre-training of Deep Bidirectional Transformers for Language Understanding". In: *Proceedings of the 2019 Conference of the North American Chapter of the Association for Computational Linguistics: Human Language Technologies (NAACL-HLT)*. 2019, pp. 4171–4186.

[6] Ahmed Elgohary, Denis Peskov, and Jordan Boyd-Graber. "Can You Unpack That? Learning to Rewrite Questions-in-Context". In: *Proceedings of the 2019 Conference on Empirical Methods in Natural Language Processing and the 9th International Joint Conference on Natural Language Processing (EMNLP-IJCNLP)*. 2019, pp. 5918–5924.

[7] Jianfeng Gao, Michel Galley, and Lihong Li. "Neural Approaches to Conversational AI". In: *Foundations and Trends in Information Retrieval* 13 (2019).

[8] Hsin-Yuan Huang, Eunsol Choi, and Wen-tau Yih. "FlowQA: Grasping Flow in History for Conversational Machine Comprehension". In: *Proceedings of the 7th The International Conference on Learning Representations*. 2019, pp. 86–90.

[9] Etsuko Ishii et al. "Integrating Question Rewrites in Conversational Question Answering: A Reinforcement Learning Approach". In: *Proceedings of the 60th Annual Meeting of the Association for Computational Linguistics (ACL)*. 2022, pp. 55–66.

[10] Gangwoo Kim et al. "Learn to Resolve Conversational Dependency: A Consistency Training Framework for Conversational Question Answering". In:

Proceedings of the 59th Annual Meeting of the Association for Computational Linguistics and the 11th International Joint Conference on Natural Language Processing (ACL-IJCNLP). 2021, pp. 6130–6141.

[11] Mike Lewis et al. "BART: Denoising Sequence-to-Sequence Pre-training for Natural Language Generation, Translation, and Comprehension". In: *Proceedings of the 58th Annual Meeting of the Association for Computational Linguistics (ACL).* 2020, pp. 7871–7880.

[12] Huihan Li et al. "Ditch the Gold Standard: Re-evaluating Conversational Question Answering". In: *Proceedings of the 60th Annual Meeting of the Association for Computational Linguistics (ACL).* 2022, pp. 8074–8085.

[13] Sheng-Chieh Lin et al. "Conversational Question Reformulation via Sequence-to-Sequence Architectures and Pretrained Language Models". In: *CoRR* abs/2004.01909 (2020).

[14] Yinhan Liu et al. "RoBERTa: A Robustly Optimized BERT Pretraining Approach". In: *CoRR* abs/1907.11692 (2019).

[15] Yasuhito Ohsugi et al. "A Simple but Effective Method to Incorporate Multi-turn Context with BERT for Conversational Machine Comprehension". In: *Proceedings of the 57th Annual Meeting of the Association for Computational Linguistics (ACL).* 2019, pp. 11–17.

[16] Minghui Qiu et al. "Reinforced History Backtracking for Conversational Question Answering". In: *Thirty-Fifth AAAI Conference on Artificial Intelligence (AAAI).* 2021, pp. 13718–13726.

[17] Chen Qu et al. "Attentive History Selection for Conversational Question Answering". In: *Proceedings of the 28th ACM International Conference on Information*

and Knowledge Management (CIKM). 2019, pp. 1391–1400.

[18] Chen Qu et al. "BERT with History Answer Embedding for Conversational Question Answering". In: *Proceedings of the 42nd International ACM Conference on Research and Development in Information Retrieval (SIGIR)*. 2019, pp. 1133–1136.

[19] Alec Radford et al. "Improving Language Understanding by Generative Pre-training". In: *OpenAI Blog* 2.5 (2018).

[20] Gonçalo Raposo et al. "Question rewriting? Assessing its importance for conversational question answering". In: *Proceedings of 44th European Conference on Information Retrieval (ECIR)*. 2022, pp. 199–206.

[21] Siva Reddy, Danqi Chen, and Christopher D. Manning. "CoQA: A Conversational Question Answering Challenge". In: *Transaction of Association for the Computational Linguistics 7* (2019), pp. 1–8.

[22] Svitlana Vakulenko et al. "A Wrong Answer or a Wrong Question? An Intricate Relationship between Question Reformulation and Answer Selection in Conversational Question Answering". In: *Proceedings of the 5th International Workshop on Search-Oriented Conversational AI (SCAI)*. 2020, pp. 7–16.

[23] Svitlana Vakulenko et al. "Question Rewriting for Conversational Question Answering". In: *Proceedings of the 14th ACM International Conference on Web Search and Data Mining (WSDM)*. 2021, pp. 355–363.

[24] Svitlana Vakulenko et al. "Question Rewriting for Conversational Question Answering". In: *Proceedings of the 14th ACM International Conference on Web Search and Data Mining (WSDM)*. 2021, pp. 355–363.

[25] Nikos Voskarides et al. "Query Resolution for Conversational Search with Limited Supervision". In: *Proceedings of the 43rd Annual International ACM Conference on Research and Development in Information Retrieval (SIGIR)*. 2020.

[26] Yi-Ting Yeh and Yun-Nung Chen. "FlowDelta: Modeling Flow Information Gain in Reasoning for Conversational Machine Comprehension". In: *Proceedings of the 2nd Workshop on Machine Reading for Question Answering*. 2019, pp. 86–90.

[27] Shi Yu et al. "Few-shot Generative Conversational Query Rewriting". In: *Proceedings of the 43rd International ACM Conference on Research and Development in Information Retrieval (SIGIR)*. 2020, pp. 1933–1936.

[28] Munazza Zaib et al. "BERT-CoQAC: BERT-based Conversational Question Answering in Context". In: *Proceeding of International Symposium on Parallel Architectures, Algorithms and Programming (PAAP)*. 2021, pp. 47–57.

[29] Munazza Zaib et al. "Conversational Question Answering: A Survey". In: *Knowledge and Information Systems* 64.12 (2022).

[30] Munazza Zaib et al. "Keeping the Questions Conversational: Using Structured Representations to Resolve Dependency in Conversational Question Answering". In: *International Joint Conference on Neural Networks (IJCNN)*. 2023, pp. 1–7.

CHAPTER 4

Dynamic History Selection for Conversational Question Answering

The increasing demand for web-based digital assistants has given a rapid rise in the interest of the IR community toward the field of ConvQA [4]. However, one of the critical aspects of ConvQA is the effective selection of conversational history turns to answer the question-at-hand [5, 25]. The dependency between relevant history selection and correct answer prediction is an intriguing but under-explored area. The selected relevant context can better guide the system to where exactly in the passage to look for an answer. Irrelevant context, on the other hand, brings noise to the system [28], thereby resulting in a decline in the model's performance. This chapter is an effort to dynamically incorporate and model the relevant context to address the aforementioned issue. The proposed framework first generates the context and question entities for all the history turns, which are then pruned based on the similarity they share in common with the question at hand. It also utilizes

DOI: 10.1201/9781003592068-4

an attention-based mechanism to re-rank the pruned terms based on their calculated weights of how useful they are in answering the question. In the end, the model is further aided by highlighting the terms in the re-ranked conversational history using a binary classification task keeping the useful terms (predicted as 1) and ignoring the irrelevant terms (predicted as 0). We demonstrate the efficacy of the proposed framework with extensive experimental results on CANARD and QuAC – the two popularly utilized datasets in ConvQA. We also demonstrate that selecting relevant turns works better than rewriting the original question and investigate how adding the irrelevant history negatively impacts the model's performance.

4.1 OVERVIEW

The long-standing objective of the IR community has been to design intelligent agents, whether web-based or mobile-based, that can engage in eloquent interaction with humans iteratively [9, 7, 29]. The IR community has come closer to the realization of the dream owing to the rapid progress in conversational datasets and pre-trained language models [29]. These advancements have resulted in the birth of the field of ConvQA. ConvQA provides a simplified but strong setting for conversational search [15], where the user initiates the conversation with a specific information need in mind. The system attempts to find relevant information pertinent to the question at hand iteratively based a user's response or follow-up questions [15, 27, 14]. When answering the follow-up questions, the model needs to take the previous conversational turns into account to comprehend the context [18, 1]. Selecting the relevant context that helps the model in building a clear and strong understanding of the current question is, therefore, a very critical challenge in ConvQA [14, 13, 28]. Adding the entire conversational history may bring noise to the system with irrelevant context. This hinders the model's capability to correctly interpret the context of the conversation [19, 28], thus resulting in a decline in the accuracy of the predicted answer.

The process of selecting the relevant conversational turns and predicting the correct answer span is based on several factors. The flow of conversation keeps on changing because of the presence of dialog features like dialog shift, topic return, drill down, and clarification [24]. Therefore, prepending k immediate turns, as suggested in [15, 31, 20, 12], will not be able to capture the gist of what the current question is about. Table 4.1 shows an example of a conversational excerpt. Q2 shows a *topic shift*, whereas Q3 represents *topic return*. Q4 and Q5 are examples of topic drill. The topic of Q4 is related to the band. Adding Q2, which inquires about the singer, to it would introduce noise within the input.

Another factor is incomplete or vague follow-up questions that impede the model from fully interpreting the conversation to be able to select the relevant conversational turns. The literature [17, 6, 22, 26] suggests the task of QR to address the issue where QR refers to rewriting the current question by adding missing information or resolving co-references, thereby, making it context-independent [17]. However, taking questions out of the conversational context results in losing important cues from the conversational flow. Also, the rewritten questions might be lengthy and verbose which, in turn, adds difficulty in selecting relevant conversational history [2]. The model requires the resolution of "it" and information about missing context (i.e., the band) to extract the answer span of Q4 from Table 4.1.

This chapter proposes a framework, DHS-ConvQA (*Dynamic History Selection in Conversational Question Answering*), that focuses on selecting the relevant conversational turns by ensuring the changing conversational flow and incomplete information requirement expressed in the query in view. The model first generates the context entities and question entities for the entire conversational history using distant supervision learning. The *context entity* refers to the entity mentioned from the conversational

TABLE 4.1   An Example of Information-Seeking
Conversation

Topic: Jal-The band	
ID	**Conversation**
Q1	Who founded Jal?
A1	Goher Mumtaz and Atif Aslam.
Q2	Where was Atif Aslam born?
A2	Wazirabad
Q3	When was the band founded?
A3	2002.
Q4	What was their first album?
A4	Aadat.
Q5	When was it released?

The relevant terms in the conversational history are highlighted
in boldface.

context, whereas *question entity* is the entity targeted in the
current question. Once the entities are generated, the turns
containing non-similar context entities and question entities
as compared to the current question are pruned. The remaining conversational turns are then re-ranked based on their
relevance to the current question. Their relevance is measured via the weightage assigned to them using the history
attention mechanism. In the end, to further aid the answer
prediction process, we utilize a binary classification task to
highlight the key terms within the conversation history as
1 and 0. This particularly helps the model with the incomplete questions by providing hints about what the current
question is about. The proposed framework has been compared to the standard QR module to evaluate its effectiveness. Thus, the main contributions of this chapter are as
follows:

1. A distant supervision approach to generate context
   and question entities for conversational turns has
   been proposed. The turns that do not share similar

context and question entities to the current question are pruned. The remaining turns are then re-ranked based on their relevance to the question.

2. The model uses binary term classification to highlight the important information from the conversational history. This helps in adding the missing information to the current incomplete question so that the model gets a better picture of the conversational flow.

3. The experimental setup demonstrates that the dynamic history selection works better than QR and that the presence of negative samples or irrelevant turns results in a decline in the model's performance.

The remainder of the chapter is organized as follows: Section 4.2 delineates the existing ConvQA attempts to incorporate the relevant context. Sections 4.3 presents the proposed history selection framework for ConvQA, and Sections 4.4 and 4.5 report the simulation setup and the performance analysis of the proposed model. Finally, Section 4.6 gives the concluding remarks.

4.2 STATE OF THE ART

4.2.1 Conversational Question Answering

ConvQA is still in its infancy and has several critical challenges that demand attention. One such challenge is the selection of the relevant history turns and how to utilize them within the framework [14, 28]. The approaches within extractive ConvQA utilize static and dynamic methods to represent conversational history. In the case of the static history representation methods, the widely used approach involves prepending k history turns to the current question [18, 1, 20]. On the contrary, the dynamic selection can be further categorized as *hard history selection* and *soft history selection*. *Hard history selection* is a mechanism to select a subset of question-relevant conversational turns [15, 13, 28]. However, the more pervasive and reliable method is to generate question-aware contextualized representations of the conversational history [5, 14]. The contextualized representations are, then, passed on to the neural reader to look for the answer span within the given context passage. A combination of the two techniques (i.e., *soft and hard history selection*) has been utilized to filter out the irrelevant turns and utilize only the relevant conversational history within the model.

This work also encompasses the field of QR and the related work to it is already discussed in Section 3.2 of Chapter 3.

4.3 METHODOLOGY

4.3.1 Task Formulation

The research work conducted in this chapter considers the traditional setting on ConvQA wherein a user instigates the conversation with a specific information need and the system attempts to provide a relevant and accurate answer after each of the user's questions [28]. To answer each question, the model needs to refer to the previous conversation turns to get the quintessence of the context of the conversation [28, 13, 15]. However, not all the previous turns contribute to aiding the model in understanding the current question. Thus, the proposed model follows a four-step process to make sure that the most relevant terms are selected from the entire conversation and those selected turns maximize the probability of correct answer prediction by providing additional cues to the answer prediction module.

Formally, given a context passage C, current question Q_i, previous history turns H, the task of our proposed framework is to select the most relevant history turns H' based on different factors such as having similar context and question entities to the question at hand and the order based on their weightage which shows their relevance to the question. Once the conversational turns are selected, we further aid the answer prediction process by highlighting the relevant terms using the classification task.

4.3.2 Pipeline Approach

One of the most common techniques that have been in use to tackle the complexity of ConvQA tasks is by decomposing it into two sub-tasks of QR and QA [6, 23, 17, 21]. The output from the QR module serves as an input to the QA module. The QR module is responsible for re-generating the question from scratch based on the provided context and the question at hand. Different techniques are in practice to produce these rewrites such as neural networks [23] and pre-trained language models [17, 21, 10].

The QR module can be trained on CANARD [3] dataset that consists of context-independent rewrites of the QuAC [1] dataset. The dataset contains 40K question-answer pairs produced by human annotators. Similar to [10], we utilize GPT-2 [16] to train the QR module. The conversational turns and the current question are passed on as input to the module during the training process and the module is required to generate a question rewrite that is to be answered by the QA module. Since it is assumed that all the dependencies and co-references have been resolved when rewriting the question, we use a traditional QA model instead of a ConvQA model to answer the question. We put together the process of predicting an answer as follows:

$$P(a_i \mid q_i, C, H) \approx P^{qa}(a_i \mid P^{qr}(q'_i \mid qi, H), C) \qquad (4.1)$$

where P^{qa} and P^{qr} represent the probability of the two sub-task modules, respectively. q'_i represents the rewritten question by the QR module and will be provided as input to the QA module along with conversational history as shown in Figure. 4.1a.

(a) Pipeline approach

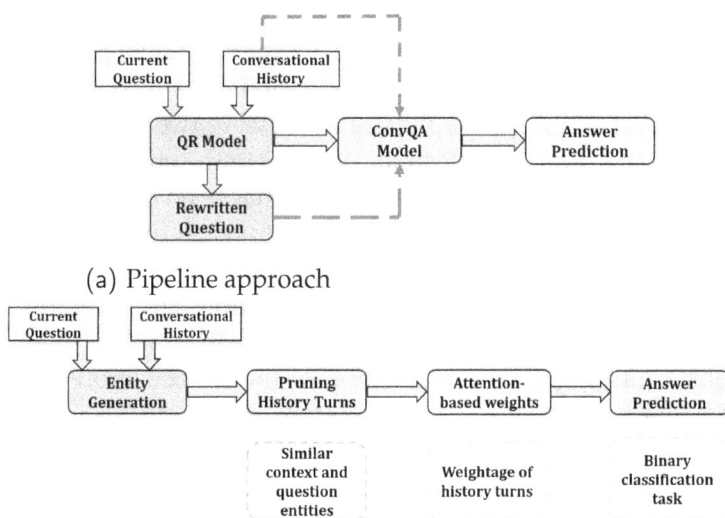

(b) The proposed approach

FIGURE 4.1   In the traditional pipeline approach shown in (a), a context-independent question rewrite is generated by the QR module that is then answered by the QA module. The illustration of the proposed framework in (b) shows the dotted line modules that aid the respective process and help the model in finding relevant conversational turns that can help predict the correct answer span.

4.3.3   DHS-ConvQA

The task of retrieving the curated context is challenging and most of the existing approaches [25, 5, 15, 14, 12] fail to address this significant aspect. They either use "hard history selection" by prepending k conversational turns or utilize "soft history selection" by focusing more on relevant context. To the best of our knowledge, the idea of filtration of irrelevant context is still unexplored. To tackle this challenge, the idea of combining both strategies has been investigated.

ConvQA heavily relies on conversational history. The more relevant and curated the conversational history is presented as input, the higher the chances of predicting the correct answer span. In the proposed method, we focus on utilizing different techniques to select the most relevant conversational turns to help the model better understand the question at hand. We emphasize addressing two issues. The first is to identify the relevance of turns to the current question. For this, the idea from Chapter 4 has been extended to generate context and question entities for each turn. To capture these entities for any incomplete question, the context and question entities from the last question have been utilized. The underlying intuition is that the incomplete questions are usually the continuation of the conversation flow and it is safe to take the information from it to fill in the missing pieces. The context entity of Q4 in Table 4.1 is **band** and the question entity is **album**. These two can easily be added to incomplete Q5 and the resultant question would be **"When was the band's album released?"**. To generate these entities, we employ a seq2seq pre-trained language model, BART [8]. The model takes the current question and the conversational history as input and is best utilized when the information is duplicated from the input but manipulated to produce the result [8]. Once the entities are generated, the next step is to prune all the history turns where there is no similarity of context and question entities with the current question. This comes under *hard history selection*.

Once the irrelevant turns are pruned, the next step is to calculate the attention weights for the remaining turns using the attention module. The attention module consists of a single-layer feed-forward network that learns an attention vector to map a sentence representation to a logit. Subsequently, the softmax probability function is utilized to calculate the probabilities across all the sequences. More formally, the computation of the weights can be shown as follows:

$$w_i = \frac{e^{D \cdot s_i^k(n)}}{\sum_{i'=1}^{I} e^{D \cdot s_i^{k'}(n)}} \tag{4.2}$$

$$\hat{t}(n) = \sum_{i'=1}^{I} t_k^i(n) \cdot w_i \tag{4.3}$$

where, D is an attention vector, s_i^k is a sentence representation, and w_i is the attention weight for s_i^k. Also, $\hat{t}(n)$ denote the aggregated token representation for the n-th token in this sequence.

Once the weights are calculated, the vectorized turns are then passed on to the next module in a sequence where the turn with the highest weight is added next to the current question. This is how *soft history selection* is utilized within the framework. The output of the attention module is then passed on to RoBERTa [11] as input. The next step is to introduce a term classification layer on top of the representations of the sub-token of each representation. The layer consists of a linear layer, a sigmoid function, and a dropout layer, and outputs a scalar value for each token. The terms relevant to the current question are highlighted as "1" and the remaining terms are set as "0". The terms represented as "1" serve as a piece of missing information for incomplete questions. Finally, the decoder will generate the answer span for the current question based on context passage, conversational history, and the additional cues added to it.

4.4 EXPERIMENTAL SETUP

4.4.1 Training of the Model

For the training of the entity generation module and binary term classification, the proposed model follows the strategy of distantly supervised labeling introduced in [2]. The idea behind the strategy is that if a piece of information is necessary for interpreting and answering the current question, it should be considered part of the current question. We start with the first question and gather all the context and question entities from it. For the incomplete or ambiguous follow-up questions, DHS-convQA keeps on adding these entities to fill in the missing information. The entities are considered to be relevant for the incomplete question if an answer is retrieved by adding them. For binary term classification, the relevant terms are tagged as 1 for being relevant and 0 for being irrelevant after passing through the term classification layer. For the task of answer prediction, the model is trained on QuAC [1] dataset.

4.4.2 Configurations

The pipeline model has been trained on around 31K pairs of original questions and their respective rewrites and validated on a development set of 3K question pairs. The test set of the QR task consists of 5K question pairs from the CANARD [3] dataset. The DHS-ConvQA model is trained, validated, and tested on around 100K question-answer pairs from QuAC [1] dataset. The entire code was written in Python, making use of the popular PyTorch library[1].

Structured representations: For generating the question and context entities, BART [8] has been utilized. The default hyperparameters were used from the Hugging Face library.[2] Early stopping was enabled with a batch size of 4. Adam optimizer with a learning rate of 0.00005 is used with a weight decay of 0.01.

Binary term classification: RoBERTa's PyTorch has been utilized in implementation by Hugging Face library[3] and introduce a term classification layer on top of it. Adam optimizer is used with a learning rate set in the range of {2e-5, 3e-5, 3e-6}. The dropout on the term classification layer lies in the range {0.1, 0.2, 0.3, 0.4}. The maximum answer length is set to 40 and the maximum question length is set to 64.

4.4.3 Dataset

The proposed model utilizes CANARD [3] and QuAC [1] datasets that have already been discussed in Section 3.4 of Chapter 3.

---

[1]https://pytorch.org/
[2]https://huggingface.co/facebook/bart-base
[3]https://huggingface.co/docs/transformers/model_doc/roberta

4.4.4 Comparison Models

As the proposed method encompasses a combination of steps, we have selectively chosen models that incorporate more or less similar components as that of the proposed technique in their models to ensure a fair comparison. The selected models are widely employed and have demonstrated exceptional performance in ConvQA settings. These methods include:

- **BERT-HAE [15]:** The BERT-based model incorporates the conversational turns with history answer embedding (HAE) to predict the correct answer span. They experimented with different conversational turn settings and found optimal answers by including five to six history turns.

- **BERT-HAM [14]:** BERT-based history answer modeling (HAM) performs *soft selection* on the relevant conversational turns. The model conducts attentive history selection based on weights assigned to them. These weights signify how relevant the turn is in answering the current question.

- **BERT-CoQAC [28]:** Instead of prepending all the conversational turns to the current question, this model utilizes cosine similarity to select the relevant turns.

- **CONVSR [30]:** The model generates the intermediate structured representations to help the model understand the current question better.

4.4.5 Evaluation Metrics

For the sake of the evaluation, the model follows the same set of metrics introduced in Section 3.3 of Chapter 3, i.e., HEQ-Q, HEQ-D, and F1 score.

TABLE 4.2 Performance Evaluation of the Pipeline Approach and the Proposed Model Using the QuAC and CANARD Datasets

Models	Approach	F1	HEQ-Q	HEQ-D
BERT-HAE	Pipeline	62.3	58.2	5.5
	Ours	**63.1** (+0.8)	**58.9** (+0.7)	**6.0** (+0.5)
BERT-HAM	Pipeline	63.4	60.1	6.1
	Ours	**65.4** (+2.0)	**61.8** (+1.7)	**6.7** (+0.6)
BERT-CoQAC	Pipeline	63.1	59.2	5.9
	Ours	**64.4** (+1.3)	**59.9** (+0.7)	**6.9** (+2.0)
CONVSR	Pipeline	66.1	62.2	6.0
	Ours	**67.5** (+1.4)	**65.3** (+3.1)	**7.5** (+1.5)

The best scores are highlighted in bold.

4.5 EXPERIMENTATION RESULTS AND ANALYSIS

The experiments are conducted using the proposed model using the QuAC [1] and CANARD [3] datasets and compare the results with the competing models.

4.5.1 DHS-ConvQA Is Viable for Selecting Relevant Conversational Turns

Topic shift and topic return are two main challenges in the field of ConvQA. Adding k immediate turns as a part of the input to the ConvQA model fails to capture the essence of the conversational flow. Also, rewriting a question takes it out of the conversational context and focuses more on generating high-quality rewrites instead of improving the performance of a ConvQA model. Thus, the first and foremost takeaway from the experimental results is that selecting relevant history turns aid the model in better understanding the question at hand and then predicting the accurate answer span. Instead of rewriting the questions to fill in the missing gaps, which takes out the questions from the conversational context, selecting relevant turns after going through different stages works well in yielding higher accuracy as shown in Table 4.2.

TABLE 4.3 The Evaluation Results of the Proposed Model
with the Competing Methods on the QuAC Dataset

Model	F1	HEQ-Q	HEQ-D
BERT-HAE	63.1	58.9	6.0
BERT-HAM	65.4	61.8	6.7
BERT-CoQAC	64.4	59.9	6.9
Ours (w/o pruning)	64.3	62.9	6.6
Ours (w/o re-ranking)	67.3	63.6	6.9
Ours (w/o term classification)	65.7	62.0	6.5
Ours (complete setup)	**67.5**	**65.3**	**7.5**

The effect of each module on the model's performance is also
demonstrated in the table.

4.5.2 Role of Relevant Conversational History in the ConvQA Setting

The existing works either opt for *soft history selection* or
employ *hard history selection*. The proposed framework employs a combination of both along with highlighting relevant
terms to the current question as additional cues. From Table 4.3, we can clearly deduce that DHS-ConvQA model consistently improves the model's performance, thereby, confirming the fact that it works well in the ConvQA setting.
We also conduct an in-depth analysis of the proposed model
by studying the effect of each module it brings within the
framework. Table 4.3 shows that omitting the pruning of
the turns step results in a greater decline in the F1 score as
compared to the other modules. The underlying reason is
that without pruning, the model considers all the conversational turns as a part of input which brings in the noise in
terms of irrelevant turns. Also, omitting the re-ranking module affects the performance of the model the least showing
that the model can still perform reasonably well given the
pruned context and highlighting the significant terms.

TABLE 4.4 The evaluation of the model's performance where the model receives Negative Samples (NS) as a part of input together with the relevant conversational turns.

Model	F1	Clarification	Topic Shift	Topic Return
Ours (complete setup)	67.5	90.9	85.4	82.2
Ours + 1NS	67.0	90.4	82.0	79.5
Ours + 3NS	64.3	89.4	78.4	77.3
Ours + 5NS	62.5	88.1	73.5	73.9
Ours + 7NS	60.7	86.7	70.9	70.3
Ours + 9NS	54.6	85.0	66.8	65.0
Ours + 11NS	52.4	83.8	63.0	62.1

4.5.3 Effect of Negative Samples on Model's Performance

For each question, we experiment by injecting negative samples together with the relevant turns identified by the proposed model. The negative samples are the questions related to the same topic but from different passages of the QuAC dataset. They are semantically closer to the relevant questions and, therefore, they can be considered a part of conversational history by the model. From Table 4.4, we can interpret that adding negative samples results in the decline of the model's F1 score. Also, the clarification questions are least impacted by the added noise as compared to the topic return and topic shift questions. The negative samples can easily be misleading for the model to capture the gist of the changing conversational flow.

4.5.4 Effect of Pruning on the Subsequent Modules In-Line

From Table 4.5, it is clearly evident that the pruning of irrelevant conversational history has a direct effect on the performance of the rest of the modules. The better the performance of the first module, the higher the chances of correct answer prediction. If the turns are pruned accurately (100%), the overall performance of all the components would be higher. The performance decreases as the number of correct pruned turns decreases. However, there are high chances of error

TABLE 4.5   Effect of pruning (in %) on the rest of the modules

Pruning (%)	Re-ranking (%)	Binary-term Classification (%)	Answer Prediction (%)
100	100	92	90
70	95	86	80
50	89	70	65

propagation because the output of each module serves as an input to the next module.

4.6   SUMMARY

This chapter discusses a significant point of view on the basic concept of the role of relevance in ConvQA. We argue that many existing research works, even the popular ones, do not take into account the idea of relevant history selection and modeling. To address this limitation, a framework has been proposed that combines the notion of both *hard history selection* and *soft history selection* to curate the input for the answer prediction module carefully. The model first generates context and question entities using distant supervision learning and selects the relevant terms using *"hard history selection"*. After the pruning of irrelevant terms, the model assigns attention-based weightage to the remaining turns. The assigned score is based on how relevant they are to the current question and accessed in the same order. To further aid the answering prediction process, we utilize binary classification task to highlight the important terms with respect to the current question from the conversational history. The experimental results depict that the proposed method has the potential to change how conversational history could be utilized more effectively.

The model presented in Section 4.3 addresses the significant issues of relevant context selection and filling up the missing information in ambiguous follow-up questions. However, the task is still far from the real-world scenario.

In real-life conversations, the users are not always provided with the gold passage and the conversation could encompass different topics in different turns of a dialog. Looking ahead to the next chapter, the goal is to extend the task of ConvQA to an open-domain setting, where the model is first required to retrieve the relevant passages based on the given question before answering it.

References

[1] Eunsol Choi et al. "QuAC: Question Answering in Context". In: *Proceedings of the 2018 Conference on Empirical Methods in Natural Language Processing (EMNLP)*. 2018, pp. 2174–2184.

[2] Philipp Christmann, Rishiraj Saha Roy, and Gerhard Weikum. "Conversational Question Answering on Heterogeneous Sources". In: *Proceedings of the 45th International ACM Conference on Research and Development in Information Retrieval (SIGIR)*. 2022, pp. 144–154.

[3] Ahmed Elgohary, Denis Peskov, and Jordan Boyd-Graber. "Can You Unpack That? Learning to Rewrite Questions-in-Context". In: *Proceedings of the 2019 Conference on Empirical Methods in Natural Language Processing and the 9th International Joint Conference on Natural Language Processing (EMNLP-IJCNLP)*. 2019, pp. 5918–5924.

[4] Jianfeng Gao, Michel Galley, and Lihong Li. "Neural Approaches to Conversational AI". In: *Foundations and Trends in Information Retrieval* 13 (2019).

[5] Hsin-Yuan Huang, Eunsol Choi, and Wen-tau Yih. "FlowQA: Grasping Flow in History for Conversational Machine Comprehension". In: *Proceedings of the 7th The International Conference on Learning Representations*. 2019, pp. 86–90.

[6]   Gangwoo Kim et al. "Learn to Resolve Conversational Dependency: A Consistency Training Framework for Conversational Question Answering". In: *Proceedings of the 59th Annual Meeting of the Association for Computational Linguistics and the 11th International Joint Conference on Natural Language Processing (ACL-IJCNLP)*. 2021, pp. 6130–6141.

[7]   Alexander Kotov and ChengXiang Zhai. "Towards Natural Question Guided Search". In: *Proceedings of the 19th International Conference on World Wide Web (WWW)*. 2010, pp. 541–550.

[8]   Mike Lewis et al. "BART: Denoising Sequence-to-Sequence Pre-training for Natural Language Generation, Translation, and Comprehension". In: *Proceedings of the 58th Annual Meeting of the Association for Computational Linguistics (ACL)*. 2020, pp. 7871–7880.

[9]   Huihan Li et al. "Ditch the Gold Standard: Re-evaluating Conversational Question Answering". In: *Proceedings of the 60th Annual Meeting of the Association for Computational Linguistics (ACL)*. 2022, pp. 8074–8085.

[10] Sheng-Chieh Lin et al. "Conversational Question Reformulation via Sequence-to-Sequence Architectures and Pretrained Language Models". In: *CoRR* abs/2004.01909 (2020).

[11] Yinhan Liu et al. "RoBERTa: A Robustly Optimized BERT Pretraining Approach". In: *CoRR* abs/1907.11692 (2019).

[12] Yasuhito Ohsugi et al. "A Simple but Effective Method to Incorporate Multi-turn Context with BERT for Conversational Machine Comprehension". In: *Proceedings of the 57th Annual Meeting of the Association for Computational Linguistics (ACL)*. 2019, pp. 11–17.

[13] Minghui Qiu et al. "Reinforced History Backtracking for Conversational Question Answering". In: *Thirty-Fifth AAAI Conference on Artificial Intelligence (AAAI)*. 2021, pp. 13718–13726.

[14] Chen Qu et al. "Attentive History Selection for Conversational Question Answering". In: *Proceedings of the 28th ACM International Conference on Information and Knowledge Management (CIKM)*. 2019, pp. 1391–1400.

[15] Chen Qu et al. "BERT with History Answer Embedding for Conversational Question Answering". In: *Proceedings of the 42nd International ACM Conference on Research and Development in Information Retrieval (SIGIR)*. 2019, pp. 1133–1136.

[16] Alec Radford et al. "Improving Language Understanding by Generative Pre-training". In: *OpenAI Blog* 2.5 (2018).

[17] Gonçalo Raposo et al. "Question rewriting? Assessing its importance for conversational question answering". In: *Proceedings of 44th European Conference on Information Retrieval (ECIR)*. 2022, pp. 199–206.

[18] Siva Reddy, Danqi Chen, and Christopher D. Manning. "CoQA: A Conversational Question Answering Challenge". In: *Transaction of Association for the Computational Linguistics* 7 (2019), pp. 1–8.

[19] Artsiom Sauchuk et al. "On the Role of Relevance in Natural Language Processing Tasks". In: *Proceedings of the 46th International ACM Conference on Research and Development in Information Retrieval (SIGIR)*. 2022, pp. 1785–1789.

[20] Min Joon Seo et al. "Bidirectional Attention Flow for Machine Comprehension". In: *5th International Conference on Learning Representations (ICLR)*. 2017.

[21] Svitlana Vakulenko et al. "A Wrong Answer or a Wrong Question? An Intricate Relationship between Question Reformulation and Answer Selection in Conversational Question Answering". In: *Proceedings of the 5th International Workshop on Search-Oriented Conversational AI (SCAI).* 2020, pp. 7–16.

[22] Svitlana Vakulenko et al. "Question Rewriting for Conversational Question Answering". In: *Proceedings of the 14th ACM International Conference on Web Search and Data Mining (WSDM).* 2021, pp. 355–363.

[23] Svitlana Vakulenko et al. "Question Rewriting for Conversational Question Answering". In: *Proceedings of the 14th ACM International Conference on Web Search and Data Mining (WSDM).* 2021, pp. 355–363.

[24] Mark Yatskar. "A Qualitative Comparison of CoQA, SQuAD 2.0 and QuAC". In: *Proceedings of the Conference of the North American Chapter of the Association for Computational Linguistics: Human Language Technologies (NAACL-HLT).* 2019, pp. 2318–2323.

[25] Yi-Ting Yeh and Yun-Nung Chen. "FlowDelta: Modeling Flow Information Gain in Reasoning for Conversational Machine Comprehension". In: *Proceedings of the 2nd Workshop on Machine Reading for Question Answering.* 2019, pp. 86–90.

[26] Shi Yu et al. "Few-shot Generative Conversational Query Rewriting". In: *Proceedings of the 43rd International ACM Conference on Research and Development in Information Retrieval (SIGIR).* 2020, pp. 1933–1936.

[27] Munazza Zaib, Quan Z. Sheng, and Wei Emma Zhang. "A Short Survey of Pre-trained Language Models for Conversational AI-A New Age in NLP". In: *Proceedings of the Australasian Computer Science Week (ACSW).* 2020, 11:1–11:4.

[28] Munazza Zaib et al. "BERT-CoQAC: BERT-based Conversational Question Answering in Context". In: *Proceeding of International Symposium on Parallel Architectures, Algorithms and Programming (PAAP)*. 2021, pp. 47–57.

[29] Munazza Zaib et al. "Conversational Question Answering: A Survey". In: *Knowledge and Information Systems* 64.12 (2022).

[30] Munazza Zaib et al. "Keeping the Questions Conversational: Using Structured Representations to Resolve Dependency in Conversational Question Answering". In: *International Joint Conference on Neural Networks (IJCNN)*. 2023, pp. 1–7.

[31] Chenguang Zhu, Michael Zeng, and Xuedong Huang. "SDNet: contextualized Attention-based Deep Network for Conversational Question Answering". In: *arXiv:1812.03593* (2018).

History Modeling for Open-Domain Conversational Question Answering

Recent research on the task of ConvQA emphasizes the role of open-retrieval in a multi-turn interaction setting consisting of a retriever-reader pipeline, wherein the former focuses on selecting relevant passages from a large collection, and the latter is required to resolve the contextual dependency to understand the question and predict the accurate answer [27, 28]. This open-domain ConvQA (OD-ConvQA) setting relies heavily on the correct retrieval of the passages, otherwise, the error propagated from the retriever module can make the reader vulnerable, thereby resulting in the model's performance degradation [16]. The existing approaches based on the retriever-reader pipeline in OD-ConvQA utilize the entire conversational context to retrieve the passages. This retrieval, however, results in the selection of irrelevant passages as well which subsequently reduces the overall performance of the model. To address the limitation, this work proposes an approach that utilizes carefully curated history turns to improve the DPR, helping the selection of more accurate answers.

The chapter solves two key challenges. First, it allows the filtration of irrelevant context from the input that limits the retrieval of entirely unrelated passages from the huge collection. Second, the model utilizes DPR, based on contrastive representation learning, which minimizes the distance between positive samples and maximizes the distance between negative ones, providing better passage representation. We validate the proposed model on two popular OD-ConvQA datasets, called OR-QuAC and TopiOCQA. The experimental result shows that the proposed model outperforms the traditional baselines and is complementary to the reader-retriever setup.

5.1 OVERVIEW

While the state-of-the-art models have achieved comparable results to human performance, the current setting of ConvQA, wherein the model requires a source paragraph to answer the question at hand, is unlike the real-world scenario. During real conversations, the gold passage is not usually available. To overcome these shortcomings, some researches [2, 28, 27, 1, 20, 16] suggests to extend the task of ConvQA to OD-ConvQA, wherein the gold passages are not provided in advance and, therefore, the model is required to retrieve the relevant passages first (as shown in Figure 5.1) and then select the correct answer span based on the conversational context. However, searching for relevant passages could be a challenging task in the open-domain setting since there could be hundreds of candidate passages, making it difficult to jointly encode the current question, contextual history, and the relevant passages [4]. DPR [18] is a recently proposed technique that is an optimal solution for tackling the issue of obtaining accurate candidate samples by encoding questions and passages separately as dense representations, and performs the similar neighbor search. However,

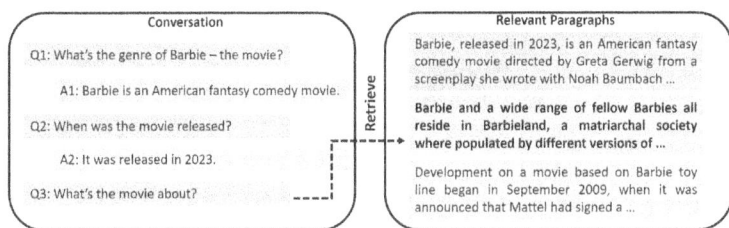

FIGURE 5.1 A sample of OD-ConvQA and example relevant passages retrieved from the collections. The gold passage for the third question is highlighted in bold.

utilizing DPR in the model requires an understanding of the conversational context. One recent research [27] has attempted to incorporate history questions as a part of the input to help the model understand the current question better. Another research [12] suggests the incorporation of history answers along with history questions so as to provide the important signal to the model to find the correct answer span. Furthermore, [31] suggests generating a rewrite of the question based on the previous context. Nevertheless, concatenating the entire conversational context is suboptimal. These methods fail to capture the essence of the question because either the question ends up losing valuable cues after being rewritten [33, 7] or some follow-up questions might be incomplete or ambiguous [19]. Besides, adding the entire context introduces noise in the form of irrelevant parts into the input, which results in degradation in the model's accuracy [25, 24]. Thus, the existing approaches can be advantaged by introducing a strategy for relevant history selection.

The chapter explores a rather under-explored research area: the task of OD-ConvQA based on DPR. It is a novel contrastive learning-based approach that aims to minimize the distance between relevant passages and maximize the distance between irrelevant ones. These passages are retrieved on the basis of curated history by comparing their relevance to the question at hand. The model selects the relevant history turns on the basis of common question and context entities they share. These captured entities can also help the model understand incomplete and ambiguous questions.

Why Conversational Context Is Necessary to Answer Questions? Conversational history or context plays a significant role in ConvQA [33, 26, 32] as it better helps the model in understanding the gist of the current question. Without the inclusion of correct conversational context, it would be difficult for the model to grasp the flow of the conversation. To aid the proposed model in getting a better idea of the posed question, we propose to provide a carefully curated subset of relevant conversational turns. This added conversational context will help the model in retrieving the passages that are relevant to the current question. The model incorporates both previous questions and answers to be the part of the input. These history turns are selected based on their relevance to the current question. The relevance is assessed based on common entities they share. We propose to capture two types of entities: (i) *question entity* and (ii) *context entity*. Question entities are the entities mentioned in the questions, whereas, context entity refers to an entity mentioned in the previous conversational context. In case of incomplete or ambiguous information, these entities from the previous turns can be utilized to understand the question better.

Role of Contrastive Learning in OD-ConvQA. For the task of OD-ConvQA, the input contains a current question, conversational history, and a collection of passages. However, there are no discrete guidelines on how to extract the current answer span from the available passages. To target this issue, a contrastive learning-based strategy has been proposed in a bid to focus on the passages that could be beneficial in answering the current question. The selected history turns and the current question would serve as a starting point in the process. Furthermore, the passage containing the answer would be considered as a *"positive sample"*, whereas the others would be treated as *"negative samples"*. Contrastive learning thus aims at learning the representations of given passages by contrasting between similar and dissimilar samples. Once the passages relevant to the context are retrieved, we utilize contrastive learning to minimize the proximity distance between the most relevant ones to better help the model understand the context and select the right answer span.

Our approach, Dense Passage Retrieval for Conversational Question Answering (DPR-ConvQA), has been validated on two publicly available datasets, namely OR-QuAC [27] and TopiOCQA [1], against the baselines. The experimental results depict that the model outperforms all of the relevant baselines. The key contributions in this work are summarized as follows:

1. A relatively new and a challenging task of OD-ConvQA has been tackled in this chapter by utilizing contrastive learning for DPR. DPR-ConvQA collectively models the relevant conversational context and collection of passages in a common space for learning joint embedding representation to improve the correct answer for the question at hand.

2. The method of relevant history selection has been utilized in the OD-ConvQA setting. This customized conversational context helps the model filter out the irrelevant passages and retrieve only those that are relevant to the given conversation. The relevance of the turns to the question is decided on the basis of context and question entities they share.

3. This chapter investigates the impact of supplying the complete conversational context on the performance of DPR-ConvQA. We demonstrate with extensive experimental results that the proposed model achieves

superior results on the relevant baselines that do not incorporate the relevant conversational context.

The rest of the chapter is organized as follows. Section 5.2 summarizes the related work. Section 5.3 presents the proposed DPR-ConvQA framework. Section 5.4 describes the experiments, including the experimental setup, datasets and metrics used, and the competing models. Section 5.5 presents the results along with the ablation studies. We offer some concluding remarks in Section 5.6.

5.2 STATE OF THE ART

The work carried out in the chapter is closely related to several research directions, including ConvQA, OD-ConvQA, and contrastive learning but we will only discuss the last two directions. The task of ConvQA has already been discussed in previous chapters. The main focus is on retrieval-based/extractive-based approaches as they yield better results than generative methods in information-seeking tasks [11].

5.2.1 Open-Domain ConvQA

Recent researches have put in a lot of effort to contribute toward the task of OD-ConvQA. Recently, Qu et al. [27] introduced a large-scale OD-ConvQA dataset, namely OR-QuAC, by extending an already existing ConvQA dataset, called QuAC [5]. They also proposed a pipeline model, called OR-ConvQA, based on retriever, re-ranker, and reader as a baseline model. Another work, ConvDR [23], experimented with TREC CAsT [8] and OR-QuAC [28] datasets by conducting a conversational search in dense embedding space. A recent research [16] focused on performing DPR using contrastive learning. Their model eliminates the reader module by directly predicting the answer phrases in the retrieval module. Recently, Fang et al. [12] presented a model, ConvADR-QA, that highlights the significance of adding history answers to the model as an input and studies its impact on the overall performance of the model.

However, one common limitation in all these approaches is the inclusion of the entire conversational context into the model. This results in the retrieval of irrelevant passages, which, in turn, leads to the incorrect answer span selection.

5.2.2 Contrastive Learning

The technique of contrastive learning focuses on learning representations of the given data by differentiating between similar and dissimilar samples [29]. Early work in contrastive learning focuses on calculating the contrastive loss for facial recognition [6]. Later on, the idea was extended and applied to different use cases such as feature clustering [6], augmented imaging [3], and DPR [15].

The work based on contrastive learning pertinent to the task of QA has been very limited. xMoCo [30] utilizes contrastive learning in an OD-QA setting to learn the question-paragraph matching where the two require separate encoders. Another recent research, PRALINE [17], exploits contrastive learning in ConvQA to rank the KG paths for retrieving the correct answers effectively. A very recent work, PRO-ConvQA [16], tackles the task of OD-ConvQA by proposing direct phrase retrieval instead of employing a traditional retriever-reader pipeline approach. The model applies contrastive learning to identify similar contextual turns and separate the irrelevant ones. This contrastive learning-based strategy helps the model to get a better understanding of the question by focusing more on the relevant context.

In the proposed research, the task is to adapt the technique of contrastive learning to maximize the distance between negative sample passages and minimize the distance between positive samples. This will help the model to better understand the question and relate it to the positive sample passages to find the accurate answer span.

5.3 METHODOLOGY

5.3.1 Task Formulation

Unlike ConvQA, the task of OD-ConvQA is required to select the relevant passages from a huge collection of passages and then retrieve the correct answer from them. Let p be the given source passage, q_i the current question, and $q_1, a_1, q_2, a_2, ..., q_n, a_n$ the given context, the task of ConvQA is to predict the answer a_i. For the sake of simplicity, we represent the entire conversational context as a concatenation of the current question and the previous history turns, which is represented as:

$$ctx_i = (q_i, q_1, a_1, q_2, a_2, ..., q_n, a_n) \qquad (5.1)$$

Thus, the task of OD-ConvQA can be formulated as:

$$f(a_i|ctx_i) = M_{OdConvQA}(p_j, ctx_i; \theta_{odconvqa}) \qquad (5.2)$$

where, $M_{OdConvQA}$ is an OD-ConvQA model parameterized by $\theta_{odconvqa}$, where p_j is the collection of the passages.

5.3.2 DPR-ConvQA

The proposed model attempts to effectively incorporate the relevant context in the retriever to guide the passage retrieval process. To the best of our knowledge, this is the first attempt to incorporate curated context within the retriever module. The overall architecture of the proposed model DPR-ConvQA is shown in Figure. 5.2. In the sequel, we will discuss the details of the two major modules of DPR-ConvQA (Algorithm 2).

5.3.2.1 *Retriever*

The input to the retriever module is the current question and the relevant history turns. To select the relevant conversation turns, we propose generating and capturing context and question entities. These entities also help complete the

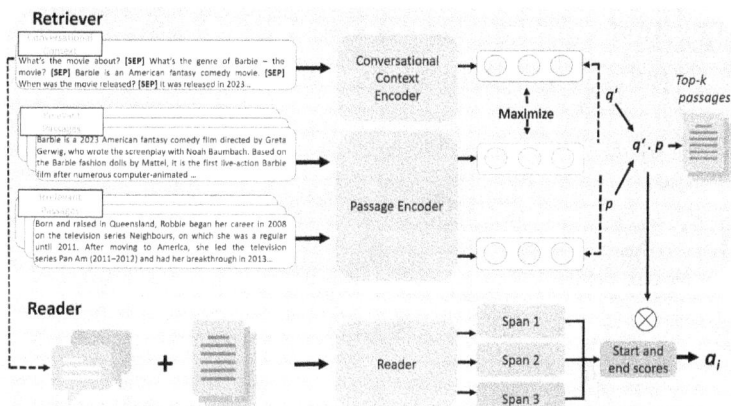

FIGURE 5.2 An illustration of the proposed model Dense Passage Retrieval for Conversational Question Answering (DPR-ConvQA), which consists of a retriever and reader modules where the output of the former serves as input to the latter.

missing information in ambiguous or incomplete questions. The idea is to generate the context and question entities for the previous turns, compare the entities of the current question to those of the previous turns, and select only those turns that share similar entities as that of the current question. If the current question is the first question in line, then the chances are that it is already complete and does not require entities to fill in the gaps.

Following the existing work in [33], a seq2seq model, BART [21], has been used, which consists of both an encoder and a decoder. The model performs best when the information is duplicated from the input but manipulated to produce the result autoregressively. BART takes the current question and the conversational context as input and generates the structured representations in the form of context and question entities as output. Once the entities are generated, the next step is to add these entities to their respective

---

Algorithm 2 The Proposed Model-DPR-ConvQA

1: **Input:** Current Question (q_i), Passage (p), History Turns (h),

2: **Output:** A: Correct Answer
   Retriever

3: $h' = relevant\ history\ turns$

4: $q' = current\ question\ along\ with\ relevant\ turns(q_i + h')$

5: $j = 1, N = Number\ of\ turns/history$

6: Capture Significant Entities from h: $CE, QE = BART(q_i[SEP]h_j^{N-1})$

7: **if** $CE, QE \notin q_i$ **then**

8: ___ h' = Prune (h)

9: **else**

10: ___ Continue

11: **end if**

12: Compute Similarity between q_i and P: $S_{ret}(q', p) = E_Q(p) \cdot E_P(q')$
   Reader:

13: $k = Number\ of\ passages\ (top\ k)$

14: **for** $k \in N$ **do**

15: ___ Compute Reader Score for Each Passage: $S_{red}(q'; p_k)$

16: **end for**

17: Compute Final Score of the Reader: $S_{final}(q', p) = S_{ret}(q', p) \cdot S_{red}(q'; p_k)$

18: $A = MAX(S_{final})$

19: **return** Correct Answer A

---

turn. These generated representations of the context are then compared to the representations of the current question, and the turns that do not share any common entity are marked as irrelevant and are pruned from the context. These representation entities are then integrated as part of the input to the reader module to provide some cues to understand the ambiguous and incomplete questions.

Following the existing work in [18], the dense passage retriever (DPR) has been utilized, which has proved to achieve better results as compared to the sparse ones. The model leverages a dual-encoder architecture to map both the passages and the selected history turns into one embedding space. The retriever score can then be calculated using the dot product of the question embeddings and the passage embeddings. At runtime, DPR utilizes different encoders to map a query and passages.

$$S_{ret}(q',p) = E_Q(p) \cdot E_P(q') \tag{5.3}$$

Training Details. The goal of the training is to generate a vector space such that the given question and the positive sample have a minimum distance between them. During the training process, each question is associated with one positive paragraph and a couple of negative paragraphs. The model is then optimized using negative log-likelihood loss which can be calculated as:

$$\mathcal{L}_{passage} = -\log \frac{e^{f(q_i, passage_+)}}{e^{f(q_i, passage_+)} + \sum_{i=1}^{B-1} e^{f(q_i, passage_{i-})}} \tag{5.4}$$

where $passage_+$ denotes positive sample and $passage_-$ represents negative samples. This loss encourages the passages similar to the question at hand to have high scores and dissimilar or negative pairs to have low scores.

Positive and Negative Passages. When it comes to the retrieval part in OD-ConvQA, the positive passages are provided explicitly, whereas the negative sample passages need to be selected from a large collection of passages. There are different strategies that can be applied for selecting irrelevant samples and the strategy can play a decisive role in learning a high-quality encoder [18]. The in-batch negatives strategy as outlined in [18] has been followed for selecting the negative samples for the model. The in-batch negatives approach assumes that we have B questions in a mini-batch and that each question is associated with a passage. Let

Q and P represent the question and passage embeddings in a batch size of B. Let S=QP^T denote the similarity matrix of size $B \times B$, wherein each row of the matrix corresponds to a question, paired with B passages. This reusing of the gold passages from the same batch as negative samples lowers the computation burden while achieving good performance. Any pair of (q_i, p_j) is considered positive when $i=j$ and is considered negative otherwise. This re-using of in-batch gold passages creates B training instances in each batch, where each question is going to have B–1 negative samples. The strategy boosts the number of training samples and has been shown to achieve good results overall [13, 14].

5.3.2.2 *Reader*

The goal of the reader module is to retrieve an accurate answer span from the relevant passages as the final answer. The traditional BERT [9] model has been utilized for the task of CMRC. Having top-k passages returned by the retriever, the task of the reader module is to select the start and end tokens bearing the highest score from each passage. Given the *top-k* passages p, conversational context along with the current question q', the reader first extracts a start and end token for each passage based on the highest score. The final answer is selected based on the product of the retriever score S_{ret} and the sum of the start and end tokens as the reader score S_{red}.

$$S_{final}(q', p) = S_{ret}(q', p) \cdot S_{red}(q'; p) \qquad (5.5)$$

5.4 EXPERIMENTAL SETUP

This section discusses the datasets used for the experiments, the evaluation metrics, the baseline models used for comparison, and the implementation details of the model.

TABLE 5.1   Hyperparameters for DPR-ConvQA

Hyperparameter	Value
Retriever	
Sequence length (question)	128
Sequence length (passage)	384
Batch size	16
Epochs	12
Learning rate	5e-5
Pre-trained embeddings	BART
Reader	
Sequence length (question)	125
Sequence length (passage)	512
Batch size	2
Epochs	3
Learning rate	5e-5
Pre-trained embeddings	BERT

5.4.1 Model Configuration

The model is implemented with PyTorch[1] and open-source implementation of BART and BERT by HuggingFace.[2] Table 5.1 presents the hyperparameters setting employed for the experiments in DPR-ConvQA. For the retriever's training, we set the maximum sequence length of the question encoder to 128, whereas 384 for the passage encoder. We use a batch size of 16, with 12 epochs, and a learning rate of 5e-5. For the reader's training, we set the maximum sequence length to 512 and the maximum question length to 125. The number of training epochs is set as three, batch size as two, and the learning rate to 5e-5. The model is trained using two NVIDIA Tesla P100 16GB GPUs.

---

[1]https://pytorch.org/
[2]https://huggingface.co/docs/transformers/index

5.4.2 Datasets

5.4.2.1 OR-QuAC

The recently introduced OR-QuAC [27] is a benchmark dataset for OD-ConvQA tasks that aggregates three other popular datasets QuAC [5], CANARD [10], and the Wikipedia dump from October 2019, and extends them to open-retrieval setting. OR-QuAC consists of around 35K conversational turns for training purposes, around 5K for testing, and 3K for validation.

5.4.2.2 TopiOCQA

Another recently introduced open-domain conversational dataset, TopiOCQA [1], focuses on topic switching between interdependent questions in conversations based on Wikipedia. The dataset consists of 3,920 conversations based on information-seeking questions and free-form answers. Each conversation has around 13 question-answer turns and the overall theme of the dataset revolves around four topics.

5.4.3 Metrics

For the sake of the evaluation, the model follows the same set of metrics introduced in Chapter 3's Section 3.3, i.e., HEQ-Q, HEQ-D, and F1 score. Following [31], we also utilize Recall and MRR to evaluate the performance of the retriever. MRR is the mean of the reciprocal ranks of all queries and Recall is the measure of the total number of relevant passages retrieved. The training and validation set has only one positive passage for each question. However, testing questions can have multiple relevant passages since there are multiple reference answers provided for each question by QuAC. The Recall evaluates whether the model can retrieve reasonably related passages for the current question. Usually, the top five passages are considered to evaluate the retriever's performance.

5.4.4 Comparison Models

- DrQA [4]: The model implements a TF-IDF-based retriever with a multi-layer RNN as a reader and is
  trained to select answers from Wikipedia passages.
  We train this model on the OR-QuAC [27] dataset
  using their open-sourced implementation available at
  GitHub.[3]

- OR-ConvQA [27]: The model consists of a retriever,
  re-ranker, and reader pipeline where it is trained in
  two phases namely, (i) retriever pre-training and (ii)
  concurrent learning. The retriever uses the dense retrieval method where the question encoder takes the
  concatenation as query and the history questions as
  input.

- ConvADR-QA [12]: The model suggests the utilization
  of history answers to select the accurate answer span
  in an ODConvQA setting.

- PRO-ConvQA [16]: The model utilizes contrastive
  learning to solve the dependencies between previous
  and current history turns within a conversation. Instead of opting for a retriever-reader pipeline, it uses
  a direct phrase prediction approach by combining the
  two subtasks into one.

- Graph-guided OD-ConvQA [22]: This work proposes
  a graph-guided based retrieval method to study the
  relationships between the previous answers in a given
  conversation. The model utilizes a passage graph that
  contains all the previous conversational answers, and a
  potential current answer to select and retrieve only relevant passages for the prediction of the correct answer
  span.

---

[3]https://github.com/facebookresearch/DrQA.

TABLE 5.2 The Evaluation Results of the Proposed Model with the Baseline Methods on the OR-QuAC and TopiOCQA datasets

Models	Retrieval		Answering		
	Recall	MRR	F1	HEQ-Q	HEQ-D
OR-QuAC					
DrQA	0.2	N/A	6.3	0.1	0.0
OR-ConvQA	31.4	31.3	29.4	24.10	0.60
PRO-ConvQA	N/A	40.0	36.84	N/A	N/A
Graph-guided OD-ConvQA	36.7	20.4	33.4	30.3	1.0
ConvADR-QA	77.9	66.8	38.4	32.11	1.16
DPR-ConvQA (ours)	**80.1**	**68.4**	**39.9**	**34.2**	**1.9**
TopiOCQA					
DrQA	0.12	N/A	5.5	0.1	0.0
OR-ConvQA	29.2	28.7	27.5	21.3	0.3
PRO-ConvQA	39.7	38.0	32.84	3.7	0.5
ConvADR-QA	75.6	63.4	35.2	30.0	1.0
DPR-ConvQA (Ours)	**77.2**	**65.3**	**35.9**	**32.6**	**1.7**

The best results are highlighted in bold. N/A indicates the unavailability of values in the respective chapter.

The experiments are conducted using the publicly available codes of the aforementioned models on GitHub[4,5,6,7] (except for Graph-guided OD-ConvQA for which the code is not available) and generated the results for the TopiOCQA dataset.

5.5 RESULTS AND DISCUSSION

This section reports the overall experimental results and presents the analysis in the discussion. We also present qualitative analysis of the proposed model in contrast to the competing models in the end.

5.5.1 DPR-ConvQA Is Viable for OD-ConvQA

Table 5.2 summarizes the main experimental results. It is evident that the proposed model, DPR-ConvQA, achieves

---

[4]https://github.com/facebookresearch/DrQA
[5]https://github.com/starsuzi/PRO-ConvQA
[6]https://github.com/MiuLab/ConvADR-QA
[7]https://github.com/prdwb/orconvqa-release

better results on both datasets compared to the other models. DrQA performs poorly as compared to the other baseline models primarily due to the performance of the reader component as the representations generated by RNN-based readers are not as good as those generated by BERT-based readers. The proposed model with relevant history manages to outperform the other baselines demonstrating that contrastive learning helps the model in narrowing down the distance between the relevant passages which, in turn, improves the chances of correct answer span selection. Since the reader module is similar to Pro-ConvQA [16], the main advantage comes from the retriever module, which based on selected history turns, retrieves the relevant passages that are further fine-tuned by contrastive learning by reducing the proximity based on similarity.

The overall result on OR-QuAC is better than the TopiOCQA dataset. The reason behind this decline in scores is that TopiOCQA has frequent topic switching and adding the entire context does not suit the task definition. On the contrary, the conversations in OR-QuAC usually revolve around similar topics and do not change often which is why the model can retrieve relevant passages from the given collection. However, DPR-ConvQA still performs better than the competing models because of its ability to capture semantic inter-relationships between passages because of contrastive learning.

5.5.2 Retriever's Performance Efficacy

To validate the role of relevant history turns in retrieving the relevant passages from the collection, we measure the retrieval performance of the baseline models in Figure 5.3. Compared to the performance of DPR-ConvQA, the other baseline models perform poorly mainly because they incorporate the entire history conversation as a part of the input. Adding irrelevant turns brings noise to the model, thereby leading to a decrease in the retriever's overall performance.

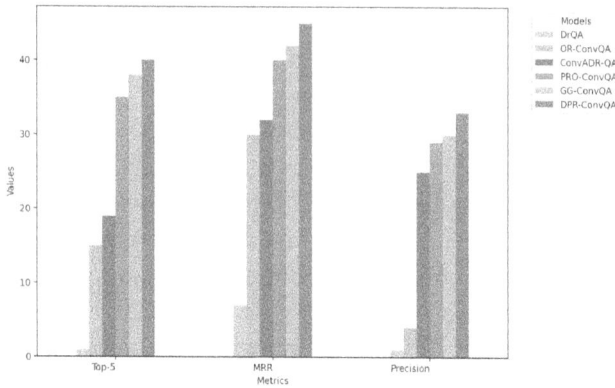

FIGURE 5.3 Retriever's results on OR-QuAC, measured with Top-5 accuracy, MRR, and precision.

The result confirms the hypothesis that there exists an issue with the current approaches where they do not implement the history selection strategy when retrieving the relevant passages. The extra history turns as an input propagates noise to the retriever stage and which, in turn, affects the overall performance of the model.

5.5.3 Effect of Retriever's Performance on Accuracy

Figure 5.4 shows the effect of the retriever's performance on the model's accuracy. DPR-ConvQA retriever module plays a significant role in improving the answering process. The better the results of the retriever module are, the higher is the accuracy of the answer span selected by the reader module. This reflects that the error propagation from the retriever module to the reader module in DPR-ConvQA was minimal as compared to the other models, thus resulting in a gain in the reader's performance.

The similarity between learned input representation and the extracted passages for Question 7 on the topic *murder of Anna Politkovskaya* has been visualized. DrQA sits in

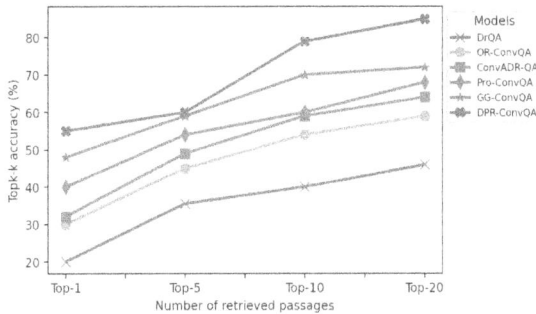

FIGURE 5.4 Accuracy evaluation on retriever's performance from different models. The scores are reported based on the context they utilize to retrieve the passages.

the middle of irrelevant passages. Since the Graph-Guided OR-ConvQA incorporates both history answers and history questions, it sits closer to the relevant passages. The same is true for ConvADR-QA and PRO-ConvQA. However, instead of relying on the entire input that might bring some noise, DPR-ConvQA only selects and incorporates the relevant turns and, which is why, it yields better performance in contrast to others. The models that have incorporated (though complete) intelligently, perform better. This shows that the better the selection and modeling of the relevant context, the more accurate would be the performance of the models.

5.5.4 Effect of Input Representations on Document Similarities

For each model, the input consists of the current question and conversational context. The learned representations generated for the input plays a significant role in extracting the relevant documents. Figure 5.5 shows that DPR-ConvQA extracts more relevant documents, whereas, DrQA performs poorly as compared to the other models.

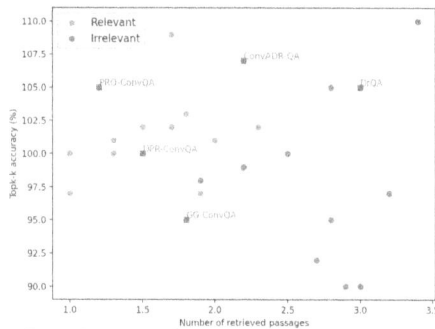

FIGURE 5.5 Similarity of query embeddings and retrieved passages for different models on the OR-QuAC dataset. The passages are denoted using a circle, whereas models are denoted by a square.

5.5.5 Role of Context on the Model Accuracy

The behavior of the proposed model is studied against baseline models at different conversational turns by reflecting their F1 accuracy score as shown in Figure 5.6. We skip the relevant history selection module in DPR-ConvQA for a fair comparison. Both history questions and answers are utilized as part of the input to the model. As depicted in Figure 5.6a, the accuracy level of the models seems to decline as the conversation grows longer. The result sits well with the idea that the longer history turns make it harder

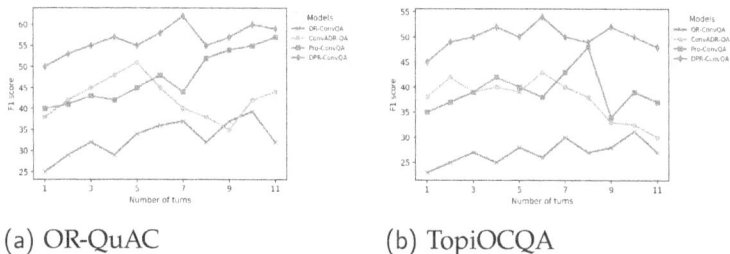

(a) OR-QuAC

(b) TopiOCQA

FIGURE 5.6 Different models' behavior at different conversational turns on the OR-QuAC and TopiOCQA datasets. TopiOCQA shows more fluctuation because of frequent topic-switching in the dataset.

for the model to resolve the conversational dependencies. The better performance of the DPR-ConvQA model comes from the fact that contrastive learning in the retriever phase provides the reader module with the edge of looking into only those documents that sit well with the conversational turns. The performance of the models on the TopiOCQA dataset is poor in comparison to the OR-ConvQA dataset, as shown in Figure 5.6b, primarily because the target passages of two consecutive conversation turns sometimes have different topics as compared to the OR-QuAC dataset, where all passages within the whole conversation share a single topic. Each conversation in TopiOCQA has 13 turns, but for the sake of fair comparison with OR-QuAC, we have truncated the last two turns to make it 11 turns in total.

5.5.6 Qualitative Comparison of the Models

The qualitative comparison of DPR-ConvQA with a recently introduced model, ConvADR-QA, is performed, and the results are presented in Table 5.3. The highlighted text in red implies that the span consisting of the ground truth answer appears in the passage. The proposed model has better performance on the two datasets making it evident that both adding selected history turns and utilizing contrastive learning for DPR provide a performance edge to the model. ConvADR-QA struggles the most in finding the right answer span in TopiOCQA as the topic keeps switching very frequently implying that adding just the history answers is not enough to select the correct answer span and a more informed context incorporation is needed to get better results. For example, Q4 from OR-QuAC dataset requires the understanding and resolution of term "he". By looking at the encoded relevant context, DPR-ConvQA was able to disambiguate it correctly, whereas ConvADR-QA couldn't return the correct answer because of the lack of proper context incorporation.

TABLE 5.3   Performance Comparison between ConvADR-QA and DPR-ConvQA on the OR-QuAC and TopiOCQA datasets

	Example 1 of an OD-ConvQA from OR-QuAC Dataset
ID	Conversation
Q1	Who worked on White Light with Clark?
A1	The album was produced by the American Indian guitarist Jesse Ed Davis, with whom Clark developed a great rapport, partly due to their common ancestry.
ConvADR-QA	Jesse Ed Davis
DPR-ConvQA	Jesse Ed Davis
Q2	Was the album a success?
A2	Launched to considerable critical acclaim, the album failed to gain commercial success, except in the Netherlands
ConvADR-QA	CANNOTANSWER
DPR-ConvQA	Failed to gain success.
Q3	What did Clark do after the failed album?
A3	In the spring of 1971, Clark was commissioned by Dennis Hopper to contribute the tracks "American Dreamer" and "Outlaw Song" to Hopper's film project American Dreamer and to Hopper's film project American Dreamer.
ConvADR-QA	CANNOTANSWER
DPR-ConvQA	Contribute the tracks American Dreamer and Outlaw Song.
Q4	Did he have any songs released in films?
A4	The Farmer.
ConvADR-QA	American Dreamer.
DPR-ConvQA	The Farmer.
	Example 2 of an OD-ConvQA from TopiOCQA Dataset
ID	Conversation
Q1	Where did typhoon Zola hit?
A1	Typhoon Zola struck Japan.
ConvADR-QA	Japan
DPR-ConvQA	Typhoon Zola struck Japan
Q2	Which cities were hit?
A2	Seven people were injured in Hiroshima Prefecture
ConvADR-QA	Hiroshima Prefecture
DPR-ConvQA	Kōchi Prefecture, Hiroshima Prefecture
Q3	what are the major economic contributors in the second place?
ConvADR-QA	CANNOTANSWER
A3	Automobiles (Mazda is headquartered there) and tourism in two World Heritage Sites
ConvADR-QA	CANNOTANSWER
DPR-ConvQA	Automobiles and tourism.

5.6   SUMMARY

This work introduces DPR-ConvQA, an OD-ConvQA model that proposes the use of selected history turns in the retriever module as part of input instead of incorporating the entire conversational context. The model is based on retriever-reader design, where the retriever employs contrastive learning to minimize the distance between similar passages and to maximize the distance of irrelevant ones. These passages along with the current question and the relevant context are then passed on to the reader module that selects the correct answer span from the retrieved passages. The extensive experiments on the OR-QuAC and TopiOCQA datasets demonstrate the significance of using relevant context when answering the questions. The experiments also show how contrastive learning can be used in OD-ConvQA to identify the relevant passages and narrow down the search space, thereby making it easier for the model to select the correct answer span. Finally, the effect of adding the entire conversational context on the proposed model's performance is studied and it demonstrates how the extra noise degrades the accuracy of the model.

References

[1] Vaibhav Adlakha et al. "TopiOCQA: Open-domain Conversational Question Answering with Topic Switching". In: *Transactions of Association for Computational Linguistics* 10 (2022).

[2] Raviteja Anantha et al. "Open-Domain Question Answering Goes Conversational via Question Rewriting". In: *Proceedings of the 2021 Conference of the North American Chapter of the Association for Computational Linguistics: Human Language Technologies, (NAACL-HLT)*. 2021, pp. 520–534.

[3] Mathilde Caron et al. "Unsupervised Learning of Visual Features by Contrasting Cluster Assignments". In: *Proceedings of the Annual Conference on Neural Information Processing Systems (NeurIPS)*. 2020.

[4] Danqi Chen et al. "Reading Wikipedia to Answer Open-Domain Questions". In: *Proceedings of the 55th Annual Meeting of the Association for Computational Linguistics (ACL)*. Ed. by Regina Barzilay and Min-Yen Kan. 2017, pp. 1870–1879.

[5] Eunsol Choi et al. "QuAC: Question Answering in Context". In: *Proceedings of the 2018 Conference on Empirical Methods in Natural Language Processing (EMNLP)*. 2018, pp. 2174–2184.

[6] Sumit Chopra, Raia Hadsell, and Yann LeCun. "Learning a Similarity Metric Discriminatively, with Application to Face Verification". In: *Proc. of 2005 IEEE Computer Society Conference on Computer Vision and Pattern Recognition (CVPR)*. 2005, pp. 539–546.

[7] Philipp Christmann, Rishiraj Saha Roy, and Gerhard Weikum. "Conversational Question Answering on Heterogeneous Sources". In: *Proceedings of the 45th ACM International Conference on Research and Development in Information Retrieval (SIGIR)*. 2022, pp. 144–154.

[8] Jeffrey Dalton, Chenyan Xiong, and Jamie Callan. "TREC CAsT 2019: The Conversational Assistance Track Overview". In: *CoRR* abs/2003.13624 (2020). arXiv: 2003.13624.

[9] Jacob Devlin et al. "BERT: Pre-training of Deep Bidirectional Transformers for Language Understanding". In: *Proceedings of the 2019 Conference of the North American Chapter of the Association for Computational Linguistics: Human Language Technologies (NAACL-HLT)*. 2019, pp. 4171–4186.

[10] Ahmed Elgohary, Denis Peskov, and Jordan L. Boyd-Graber. "Can You Unpack That? Learning to Rewrite Questions-in-Context". In: *Proceedings of the 2019 Conference on Empirical Methods in Natural Language Processing and the 9th International Joint Conference on Natural Language Processing (EMNLP-IJCNLP)*. Ed. by Kentaro Inui et al. 2019, pp. 5917–5923.

[11] Yixing Fan et al. "A Linguistic Study on Relevance Modeling in Information Retrieval". In: *Proceedings*

of the ACM Web Conference (WWW). 2021, pp. 1053–1064.

[12] Hung-Chieh Fang et al. "Open-Domain Conversational Question Answering with Historical Answers". In: *Findings of the Association for Computational Linguistics: (ACL-IJCNLP)*. 2022, pp. 319–326.

[13] Daniel Gillick et al. "Learning Dense Representations for Entity Retrieval". In: *Proceedings of the 23rd Conference on Computational Natural Language Learning (CoNLL)*. 2019, pp. 528–537.

[14] Matthew L. Henderson et al. "Efficient Natural Language Response Suggestion for Smart Reply". In: *CoRR* abs/1705.00652 (2017). arXiv: 1705.00652.

[15] Gautier Izacard et al. "Towards Unsupervised Dense Information Retrieval with Contrastive Learning". In: *CoRR* abs/2112.09118 (2021). arXiv: 2112.09118.

[16] Soyeong Jeong et al. "Phrase Retrieval for Open Domain Conversational Question Answering with Conversational Dependency Modeling via Contrastive Learning". In: *Findings of the Association for Computational Linguistics (ACL)*. 2023, pp. 6019–6031.

[17] Endri Kacupaj et al. "Contrastive Representation Learning for Conversational Question Answering over Knowledge Graphs". In: *Proceedings of the 31st ACM International Conference on Information & Knowledge Management (CIKM)*. 2022, pp. 925–934.

[18] Vladimir Karpukhin et al. "Dense Passage Retrieval for Open-Domain Question Answering". In: *Proceedings of the 2020 Conference on Empirical Methods in Natural Language Processing (EMNLP)*. 2020, pp. 6769–6781.

[19] Gangwoo Kim et al. "Learn to Resolve Conversational Dependency: A Consistency Training Framework for Conversational Question Answering". In:

Proceedings of the 59th Annual Meeting of the Association for Computational Linguistics and the 11th International Joint Conference on Natural Language Processing (ACL-IJCNLP). 2021, pp. 6130–6141.

[20] Sarawoot Kongyoung, Craig Macdonald, and Iadh Ounis. "monoQA: Multi-Task Learning of Reranking and Answer Extraction for Open-Retrieval Conversational Question Answering". In: *Proceedings of the 2022 Conference on Empirical Methods in Natural Language Processing (EMNLP)*. 2022, pp. 7207–7218.

[21] Mike Lewis et al. "BART: Denoising Sequence-to-Sequence Pre-training for Natural Language Generation, Translation, and Comprehension". In: *Proceedings of the 58th Annual Meeting of the Association for Computational Linguistics (ACL)*. 2020, pp. 7871–7880.

[22] Yongqi Li, Wenjie Li, and Liqiang Nie. "A Graph-guided Multi-round Retrieval Method for Conversational Open-domain Question Answering". In: *CoRR* abs/2104.08443 (2021). arXiv: 2104.08443.

[23] Kelong Mao, Zhicheng Dou, and Hongjin Qian. "Curriculum Contrastive Context Denoising for Few-shot Conversational Dense Retrieval". In: *Proceedings of the 45th International ACM Conference on Research and Development in Information Retrieval (SIGIR)*. 2022, pp. 176–186.

[24] Kelong Mao et al. "Learning Denoised and Interpretable Session Representation for Conversational Search". In: *Proceedings of the ACM Web Conference (WWW)*. Ed. by Ying Ding et al. 2023, pp. 3193–3202.

[25] Minghui Qiu et al. "Reinforced History Backtracking for Conversational Question Answering". In: *Proceedings of the 35th Conference on Artificial Intelligence (AAAI)*. 2021.

[26] Chen Qu et al. "BERT with History Answer Embedding for Conversational Question Answering". In: *Proceedings of the 42nd International ACM Conference on Research and Development in Information Retrieval (SIGIR)*. 2019, pp. 1133–1136.

[27] Chen Qu et al. "Open-retrieval Conversational Question Answering". In: *Proceedings of the 43rd International Conference on Research and Development in Information Retrieval (SIGIR)*. 2020, pp. 539–548.

[28] Chen Qu et al. "Weakly-Supervised Open-Retrieval Conversational Question Answering". In: *Proceedings of the 43rd European Conference on Information Retrieval Research*. 2021, pp. 529–543.

[29] Alec Radford et al. "Learning Transferable Visual Models From Natural Language Supervision". In: *Proceedings of the 38th International Conference on Machine Learning (ICML)*. Vol. 139. 2021, pp. 8748–8763.

[30] Nan Yang et al. "xMoCo: Cross Momentum Contrastive Learning for Open-Domain Question Answering". In: *Proceedings of the 59th Annual Meeting of the Association for Computational Linguistics and the 11th International Joint Conference on Natural Language Processing (ACL-IJCNLP)*. 2021, pp. 6120–6129.

[31] Shi Yu et al. "Few-Shot Conversational Dense Retrieval". In: *The 44th International ACM Conference on Research and Development in Information Retrieval (SIGIR)*. Ed. by Fernando Diaz et al. 2021, pp. 829–838.

[32] Munazza Zaib et al. "BERT-CoQAC: BERT-based Conversational Question Answering in Context". In: *Proceeding of International Symposium on Parallel Architectures, Algorithms and Programming (PAAP)*. 2021, pp. 47–57.

[33] Munazza Zaib et al. "Keeping the Questions Conversational: Using Structured Representations to Resolve Dependency in Conversational Question Answering". In: *International Joint Conference on Neural Networks (IJCNN)*. 2023, pp. 1–7.

CHAPTER 6

Conclusion and Future Directions

Despite much progress in the field of NLP and intelligent agents, the conversational part of communication between a human and a machine is still in its inception phase. It is only recently that neural generative models have gotten the attention of researchers and improved the field of ConvAI drastically. With a large amount of available "big data" and advanced deep learning methods, the objective of designing digital conversation systems as our virtual assistant is no longer a dream. This research work is a step toward enabling interactive conversations between humans and an agent by effectively modeling the relevant context. Thus, the chapter summarizes the book's findings and presents the future research directions.

6.1 BOOK SUMMARY

Motivated by the iterative and engaging features of conversational search, the role of conversational context and its effective modeling in the ConvQA-based models is studied in this work to better enable them to understand the question-at-hand and answer a user's information need. The approaches proposed in this book leverage the benefits of pre-trained language models. To the best of our knowledge, the existing ConvQA models still lack an effective incorporation of the context as a result of which the models struggle with resolving the co-dependencies between the turns. Hence, the proposed research in this book formulates ConvQA models that incorporate only relevant conversational context, thereby increasing the overall performance accuracy. Furthermore, the task of ConvQA has been extended to OD-ConvQA to make it closer to the real-world setting. The proposed work implemented the relevant history selection and modeling in the task of OD-ConvQA and studied its effect on both retrieval and correct answer extraction.

Accordingly, a comprehensive literature review is presented in Chapter 2 that starts with the definition of QA models and how ConvQA models differ from them. The discussion is further extended to highlight the two subcategories within ConvQA: (i) sequential KB-QA and (ii) conversational machine reading comprehension. A high-level overview and comparison of the ConvQA models is delineated that takes into account the different strategies utilized in their modules. The different datasets that are introduced for the task of ConvQA and their respective features have also been discussed. The chapter ends with a few identified research gaps that are still challenging and require further research.

The questions in a dialog can be incomplete or implicit and require a model to refer back to the previous turns. Chapter 3 presents our attempt to fill in missing information in ambiguous or incomplete follow-up questions. The task of QR has the potential to address the challenges of resolving dependencies among the contextual turns by transforming them into intent-explicit questions. However, this results in verbose questions, and the focus of the task shifts from ConvQA to simple QA. The technique to capture and generate intermediate representations as conversational cues has been proposed to enhance the capability of the QA model to better interpret incomplete questions. We also deliberate how the strengths of this task could be leveraged in a bid to design more engaging and eloquent conversational agents. The proposed model has been tested on the QuAC and CA-NARD datasets, and illustrates by experimental results that our proposed framework achieves a better F1 score in contrast to the standard QR model.

Chapter 4 is an effort is made to tackle the problem of irrelevant context identified in Chapter 3. It is an attempt to incorporate dynamic history selection based on its relevance to the current question in a ConvQA model. The motivation behind this idea is adding irrelevant turns introduces noise in the model which, in turn, results in a model's performance degradation. Also, the smaller the size of the input, the lower would be the computational overhead. The proposed approach first generates the context and question entities for all the history turns, and which are then pruned based on the similarity they share in common with the question-at-hand. An attention-based mechanism has also been proposed to re-rank the pruned terms based on their calculated weights of how useful they are in answering the question. In the end, the model has been further aided by highlighting the terms in the re-ranked conversational history using a binary classification task keeping the useful terms (predicted as 1) and ignoring the irrelevant terms (predicted as 0). The efficacy of the proposed framework is demonstrated with extensive experimental results on CANARD and QuAC—the two popularly utilized datasets in ConvQA. Selecting relevant turns is shown to yield better results than rewriting the original question.

Chapter 5 is an attempt to take the task of ConvQA closer to the real-world setting by extending it to OD-ConvQA. In OD-ConvQA, the model learns to retrieve the relevant passages before extracting the correct answer span. This adds an extra step of retrieval and the task is usually carried out using the retriever-reader pipeline. The retrieval, however, results in the selection of irrelevant passages as well and which subsequently reduces the overall performance of the model. To address this limitation, a strategy that utilizes carefully curated history turns has been proposed to improve the DPR, thereby helping the selection of more accurate answers. Our approach solves two key challenges. First, it allows the filtration of irrelevant context from the input that limits the retrieval of entirely unrelated passages from a huge collection. Second, the model utilizes DPR, based on contrastive representation learning, which minimizes the distance between positive samples and maximizes the distance between negative ones, in turn, providing better passage representation. The proposed model has been validated on two popular OD-ConvQA datasets, OR-QuAC and TopiOCQA. The experimental results show that the proposed method outperforms the traditional baselines and is complementary to the reader-retriever setup.

6.2   FUTURE RESEARCH DIRECTIONS

As an emerging research area with many significant promising applications, ConvQA techniques are still not mature yet and mandate further attention. In this section, several key open research issues have been discussed.

6.2.1   The Role of Contextual Dynamics in ConvQA

The role of context to be selected plays a significant role in providing accurate answers in ConvQA. With richer conversational scenarios, several contextual features need to be considered, including personal context, social context, and task context. General research questions regarding contextual information in ConvQA include the following: *"What are the effective strategies and models to collect and integrate contextual information?"*, *"Are knowledge graphs sufficient enough to capture and represent this information?"*, and *"Do we need to incorporate the entire context or a relevant chunk would be enough to find the correct answer?"*.

Different models attempt to incorporate context in different ways. Out of all the history selection methods, the dynamic history selection mechanism proposed by Qu et al. [12] is more compelling and intuitive. As far as the flow-methods are concerned, they consider the latent representations of the entire context to deal with the varying conversational aspect. Similarly, for sequential KB-QA, the authors in [3] proposed the use of dialog manager to collect and maintain the previous utterances. Another approach [10] utilizes reinforcement learning and a user's feedback to better guide the history selection process.

6.2.2 Mitigating Error Propagation in OD-ConvQA

Error propagation is very common for many NLP tasks. It can occur within the application of a specific task when sequential decisions are taken and errors made early in the process affect decisions made later on. Most of the existing research works in OD-ConvQA utilize a retriever-reader pipeline to tackle the task. However, utilizing such an experimental setup results in error propagation from the retriever to the reader module.

A few different approaches have suggested different strategies to tackle the issue of error propagation. One recent work [20] suggests the use of Large Language Models (LLMs) to first generate the passages based on the given question and then retrieve the more relevant passages. This generation of passages based on a given question substantially reduce the chances of irrelevant passages being retrieved. Another recent work [5] suggests phrase retrieval, rather than answer spans extraction after the retrieval phase to mitigate the chances of error propagation.

6.2.3 User Intent Identification

Apart from utilizing conversational context, other conversational cues could also play a significant part in helping the ConvQA model select the correct answer span. One such feature is intent identification that provides additional information to the model about the information needs of a user. Researchers at different conferences, such as WSDM'18[1] and SIGIR'17[2], have pointed out the significant need for user intent analysis. Once a user's intention is correctly identified, it can help greatly in providing customized recommendations, targeted advertising, optimized customer support, etc. This, in turn, results in increased customer loyalty.

Incorporating external information could play a vital role in predicting a user's intent. A research work [11] proposed a labeled dataset for user intent identification in ConvQA domain. They also proposed an approach where they incorporated features such as sentiments, content, and structures to see how they contribute to intent prediction. Another popular work [13] proposed an enhanced neural classifier to incorporate context to predict a user's intention.

6.2.4 Modeling Information-Seeking Behaviors in ConvQA

Information-seeking behaviors need to be modeled for the ConvQA setting as it provides users with an opportunity to obtain more information about the topics of their interests. The research questions related to information-seeking behaviors that need to be explored include: *"What optimal structure for clarification questions can be used to better understand the users' information need?"* and *"What effective strategies can be employed to design such clarification questions?"*. These clarification or follow-up questions play a significant role in helping the model understand the information needs of a user.

Existing research has attempted diverse approaches to enhance the quality of clarification questions. However, owing to the lack of authentic conversational search data, these approaches rely on artificial datasets for training, thereby restricting their applicability to real-world search scenarios.

---

[1]https://www.wsdm-conference.org/2018/
[2]https://sigir.org/sigir2017/

One recent research [19] attempted this cold-start by implementing zero-shot setting, wherein the model uses both question templates and query facets to guide the effective and precise question generation.

6.2.5 Enhancing Inference in ConvQA

Lack of inference capability is one of the reasons why QA struggles with generating the correct answers. Most of the existing ConvQA systems are based on semantic relevance between a question and the given context which limits a model's capability to reason. An example discussed by Liu et al. [7] depicts that provided the context, *"five people on board and two people on the ground died"*, the system was not able to provide the correct answer, *"seven"*, to the question, *"how many people died?"*. Thus, how to design systems with strong inference ability is still an open issue and calls for further research.

In the existing ConvQA systems, the models are anticipated to provide the answers to the questions without having to explain as to why and how they deduced an answer, thereby making it difficult to understand the source and reason for an answer. CoQA [15] is the only ConvQA dataset that provides reasoning for the provided answer. Another model, Cos-E [14], generates commonsense reasoning explanations for the deduced answer. Whether or not the complete interpretability of ConvQA models is required, we can safely say that an understanding of the working of the internal model to a certain extent can greatly help and improve the design of neural network systems in the future. A very recent work, EXPLAIGNN [2], is an attempt to provide a user with comprehensible explanations along with integrating different sources to come up with the needed information.

6.2.6 Unraveling Commonsense Reasoning in ConvAI

Commonsense reasoning is a long-standing challenge in ConvAI, i.e., whether it is incorporating commonsense in dialog systems or QA systems. Commonsense reasoning refers to the ability of an individual to make day-to-day inferences by using or assuming basic knowledge about the real-world. However, the ConvQA systems proposed so far work on pragmatic reasoning, i.e., finding the intended meaning(s) from the provided context because common-sense knowledge is often not explicitly explained in the data sources (i.e., KB-QA or CMRC dataset).

Despite single-turn QA systems almost achieving human-level performance, the implementation of common-sense reasoning is still not very common. There are only a few research works that take commonsense reasoning into consideration when performing single-turn QA [9, 4]. There has been an increasing trend to incorporate commonsense reasoning into the single-turn MRC over the past few years. However, when it comes to utilizing commonsense reasoning in CMRC, no successful attempt has been made. This may probably be because commonsense reasoning requires questions that need some prior knowledge or background which the current CMRC datasets do not provide. Neverthe-less, a recently introduced work, BlenderBot3 [17], is capable of performing some level of commonsense reasoning. It is an open-domain dialog agent, designed by Meta, to carry out smooth and natural conversations and is based on OPT [21], an open source model comparable to GPT-3.

In single-turn KB-QA, there are a number of promi-nent researches that utilize commonsense in a QA process [6, 8]. Another effort was made by CoMET [1], wherein a transformer to generate commonsense knowledge graphs was employed. Knowledge graphs like ConceptNet [18] and ATOMIC [16] have been designed to facilitate the imple-mentation of commonsense in KB-QA systems. The field of sequential KB-QA remains untouched primarily because of the reason that the majority of existing methods lack the absence of connections between concepts [22].

References

[1] Antoine Bosselut et al. "COMET: Commonsense Transformers for Automatic Knowledge Graph Construction". In: *Proceedings of the 57th Annual Meeting of the Association for Computational Linguistics (ACL)*. 2019, pp. 4762–4779.

[2] Philipp Christmann, Rishiraj Saha Roy, and Gerhard Weikum. "Explainable Conversational Question Answering over Heterogeneous Sources via Iterative Graph Neural Networks". In: *Proceedings of the 46th International ACM Conference on Research and Development in Information Retrieval (SIGIR)*. 2023, pp. 643–653.

[3] Daya Guo et al. "Dialog-to-Action: conversational Question Answering Over a Large-Scale Knowledge Base". In: *Proceedings of the 32nd International Conference on Neural Information Processing Systems (NeurIPS)*. 2018, pp. 2946–2955.

[4] Lifu Huang et al. "Cosmos QA: Machine Reading Comprehension with Contextual Commonsense Reasoning". In: *Proceedings of the Conference on Empirical Methods in Natural Language Processing and the 9th International Joint Conference on Natural Language Processing (EMNLP-IJCNLP)*. 2019, pp. 2391–2401.

[5] Soyeong Jeong et al. "Phrase Retrieval for Open Domain Conversational Question Answering with Conversational Dependency Modeling via Contrastive Learning". In: *Findings of the Association for Computational Linguistics (ACL)*. 2023, pp. 6019–6031.

[6] Bill Yuchen Lin et al. "KagNet: Knowledge-Aware Graph Networks for Commonsense Reasoning". In: *Proceedings of the Conference on Empirical Methods in Natural Language Processing and the 9th International Joint Conference on Natural Language Processing (EMNLP-IJCNLP)*. 2019, pp. 2829–2839.

[7] S. Liu et al. "R-Trans: RNN Transformer Network for Chinese Machine Reading Comprehension". In: *IEEE Access* 7 (2019), pp. 27736–27745.

[8] Shangwen Lv et al. "Graph-Based Reasoning over Heterogeneous External Knowledge for Commonsense Question Answering". In: *Proceeding of the 34th Conference on Artificial Intelligence (AAAI)*. 2020, pp. 8449–8456.

[9] Simon Ostermann et al. "MCScript: a Novel Dataset for Assessing Machine Comprehension Using Script Knowledge". In: *Proceedings of the 11th International Conference on Language Resources and Evaluation (LREC)*. 2018, pp. 01–08.

[10] Minghui Qiu et al. "Reinforced History Backtracking for Conversational Question Answering". In: *Proceedings of the 35th Conference on Artificial Intelligence (AAAI)*. 2021.

[11] Chen Qu et al. "Analyzing and Characterizing User Intent in Information-seeking Conversations". In: *Proc. of the 41st International ACM Conference on Research & Development in Information Retrieval (SIGIR)*. 2018, pp. 989–992.

[12] Chen Qu et al. "Attentive History Selection for Conversational Question Answering". In: *Proceedings of the 28th ACM International Conference on Information and Knowledge Management (CIKM)*. 2019, pp. 1391–1400.

[13] Chen Qu et al. "User Intent Prediction in Information-seeking Conversations". In: *Proceedings of the 2019 Conference on Human Information Interaction and Retrieval (CHIIR)*. 2019, pp. 25–33.

[14] Nazneen Fatema Rajani et al. "Explain Yourself! Leveraging Language Models for Commonsense Reasoning". In: *Proceedings of the 57th Conference of the*

Association for Computational Linguistics (ACL). 2019, pp. 4932–4942.

[15] Siva Reddy, Danqi Chen, and Christopher D. Manning. "CoQA: A Conversational Question Answering Challenge". In: *Transaction of Association for the Computational Linguistics 7* (2019), pp. 1–8.

[16] Maarten Sap et al. "ATOMIC: An Atlas of Machine Commonsense for If-then Reasoning". In: *Proceedings of the 33rd Conference on Artificial Intelligence (AAAI)*. Vol. 33. 01. 2019, pp. 3027–3035.

[17] Kurt Shuster et al. "BlenderBot 3: A Deployed Conversational Agent that Continually Learns to Responsibly Engage". In: *CoRR* abs/2208.03188 (2022). arXiv: 2208.03188.

[18] Robyn Speer, Joshua Chin, and Catherine Havasi. "ConceptNet 5.5: An Open Multilingual Graph of General Knowledge". In: *Proceedings of the 31st Conference on Artificial Intelligence (AAAI)*. 2017, pp. 4444–4451.

[19] Zhenduo Wang et al. "Zero-shot Clarifying Question Generation for Conversational Search". In: *Proceedings of the ACM Web Conference (WWW)*. 2023, pp. 3288–3298.

[20] Wenhao Yu et al. "Generate rather than Retrieve: Large Language Models are Strong Context Generators". In: *Procceding of the 11th International Conference on Learning Representations (ICLR)*. 2023.

[21] Susan Zhang et al. "OPT: Open Pre-trained Transformer Language Models". In: *CoRR* abs/2205.01068 (2022). arXiv: 2205.01068.

[22] Wanjun Zhong et al. "Improving Question Answering by Commonsense-Based Pre-training". In: *Proceedings of the 8th International Natural Language Processing and Chinese Computing Conference (NLPCC)*. 2019, pp. 16–28.

Index